Thanks for your support -

[signature]

May 2000

A Time for Leadership

GLOBAL PERSPECTIVES FROM AN ACCELERATED EUROPEAN MARKET PLACE

by John R. Childress

Los Angeles, New York, London

A Leadership Press book, published by arrangement with the
authors.

Leadership Press
Los Angeles, New York

Library of Congress Catalog Card Number: 00-100351

Childress, John R.
A Time for Leadership: Global Perspectives from an Accelerated European Marketplace

Includes index.

Introduction. 1. The Emerging European Landscape. 2. New
Principles for Leadership in 21st Century Europe. 3. Distributed Leadership. 4. Culture Impacts Performance. 5. Brand
and Culture Must Match. 6. Shadow of the Leader. 7. Balance
of Life. 8. A Leadership Agenda for the 21st Century. 9. Staying Open for Business in the New Europe.

ISBN:0-9648466-8-3

First printing, June 2000

Printed in Canada

printing number

1234567890

Copies of A Time for Leadership: Global Perspectives for an
Accelerated European Marketplace are available at special dis-
counts for bulk purchases by corporations, institutions, and
other organisations.

For more information call or contact:
Leadership Press 562-981-5251 or info_books@sdlcg.com

"The Road Not Taken" by Robert Frost, from "The Poetry of
Robert Frost", edited by Edward Connery Lathem, Henry
Holt Inc., 1969.

TABLE OF CONTENTS

Introduction

Acknowledgements

First, I would like to acknowledge that while the information for this book came from interviews with European business leaders, the summary and conclusions, and therefore any errors, are strictly my own. The sixty business leaders we interviewed were gracious enough to take time out of their busy schedules to spend a couple of hours talking to me and several of my colleagues at our firm, the Senn-Delaney Leadership Consulting Group. I hope the ideas and conclusions put forth in this book are done so in a respectful manner and are faithful to our discussions.

A book of this type is a logistic nightmare, with interviews to schedule, hundreds of letters to be written, thank you notes, and a myriad of other important activities that have taken place over the last year and a half. At the middle of this cyclone of activity was Ms. Anne Pomphrey, who as a fairly new employee at the time, raised her hand and volunteered to take on this organisational challenge. She was terrific throughout all the stages of making this book a reality. Supporting Anne with the administration and logistics was Deborah Ingram, Flavia Dalzell Payne, Tina Manuel, and Janet Rasmussen.

Several of my consulting colleagues assisted in conducting the actual face-to-face interviews and took time out of their busy schedules to do so: Ian Johnston, John Clayton, Jim Ondrus, Dustin Seale, and Lyndon Williams. Even Rena Jordan, our CFO, volunteered to conduct some of the interviews. As you can see, this process was definitely a total team effort.

Ron Schultz, our Director of Publications and Publisher, provided the time-line and the gentle (and not-so-gentle) pushing to keep things on schedule. Ron also added some key ideas when we were developing the outline and with some of the actual chapters. My writing partner, Judith Blahnik, took my unsophisticated ramblings, many of which were on audio tape, and exquisitely turned them into the phrases, style and flow of this book.

I would also like to thank Professor Grant Baird, former Chief Executive, Scottish Financial Enterprise and Ian Reid, Chief Executive of MStar. It was through meeting Professor Baird and Ian in 1997 that the initial idea of this book arose.

Many thanks to David Blacklaw, a bright MBA student in Engineering Management, for the use of some business examples from his MBA thesis.

I also want to appreciate my partner, Christiane Wuillamie for her loving support and patience. While a busy chief executive of a fast growing IT company, she made the space in our relationship that allowed me to spend numerous evenings and weekends pounding away at the computer to finish this book.

I would like to dedicate this book to my mother, Elizabeth Rader Childress, who at the time of this writing is eighty four years young! An English Literature and music teacher all her working life, she always encouraged me to express my creative side and to stand by my own thoughts and ideas.

To the business leaders of 21st century Europe, I would like to dedicate these words of Robert Frost, my favourite poet, and to ask them to reflect on their own challenges and the road ahead:

> *I shall be telling this with a sigh*
> *Somewhere ages and ages hence:*
> *Two roads diverged in a wood, and I*
> *—I took the one less travelled by,*
> *And that has made all the difference.*

Introduction

After a particularly tough day, the chief executive of a major European company came home exhausted. A barrage of crises and questions assaulted him all day. Some of these issues he was familiar with, but many he did not fully understand. Relieved to enter his own house, he slowly took off his coat, left his briefcase in the study, and made his way upstairs. Peeking into his son's room, he saw his ten-year-old playing a computer game on his PC.

The executive was amazed to see how deftly his son manoeuvred the keys. He couldn't help but notice that the game, an action sequence in which his son played the part of a helicopter pilot racing through a perilously narrow canyon, was progressing incredibly fast, with seemingly countless actions happening all at once. The slightest movements led to new situations, so the executive found it difficult to keep track of the screen activities and his son's

I have a very strong view about the European business environment that's coming, and I think it is necessary now, to face competition from America and others, to see Europe as a single market.

Peter Job,
CEO,
Reuters plc

I think there are two key points to ongoing success. The first is to have flexible staff who can adjust to the different types of environment and culture of the countries where we wish to invest and build good relationships. The second point, which is very important and I think the CEO has to follow it personally, is to avoid everybody taking for granted conventional wisdom. You have permanently to try to change the conventional wisdom and see what could be the new ideas of tomorrow before the others. Because if you discover the good ideas at the same time as your competition, you will not have the best opportunities.

Thierry Desmarest,
Chairman & CEO,
Total Fina S.A.

National boundaries and geographic divides are reducing so that the frame of reference for any business is far, far wider today than it was yesterday. And that will be even truer tomorrow. It's the challenge of wider horizons—not only in an outward sense, but also in competition entering what were your traditional areas of operations and expertise.

Brian Stewart,
Chief Executive,
Scottish & Newcastle plc

movements at the same time. He was captivated by both the speed of the game and his young son's skill.

After watching for several minutes, the executive asked his son to let him have a try. All it took was the start of one game for this Captain of Industry to discover he couldn't last even ten seconds. Try as he might, he couldn't even manoeuvre the helicopter in a straight line, let alone use the weapons systems! Before he knew what had happened, before he could make any adjustments with the controls, the helicopter had crashed three times and "Game Over!" flashed onscreen, accompanied by an ominous and unmistakable death knell. All he could do was shrug, realising he lacked the tools, skills, dexterity, and mindset to play the game. Finally, his son said, **"Dad, you can switch it to a slower speed—you know. There's a setting for beginners."**

The executive realised at once that this instrument of make-believe imitated his experience of the larger world of business. Unfortunately, there was no switch at his office to set the pace to "Slow".

The real task before this particular chief executive, and thousands of others, is to figure out ways to learn—quickly—to lead and manage in the accelerated world of 21st century Europe.

GAME OVER!

When the game changes, old skills don't always work on the new playing field. The traditional skills of planning, organising, staffing, directing and controlling—"everything they teach you in business school"—are merely foundation points. They are not survival points. If you can't play at the speed and skill level required, all you get is: **"Game Over!"**

Today's computer games, like the emerging new rules of business in 21st century Europe, are highly complex. The thinking that got us through a two– or, at best, three–dimensional world just won't work any more. The game has changed. Time is now a crucial fourth dimension. Driven by the Internet and the Information Age, **Europe is moving into Web speed now!**

Europe is powering forward into not only a pan-European marketplace, but a global marketplace. The institution of the European Union, the Euro, deregulation, cross trading, the opening of borders, and the dramatic increase of global competition have combined to create a revolutionary business climate in Europe. What's more, these sweeping changes have been accelerated by the unprecedented event known as the Internet. The result is today's business leaders face crises on a scale and in numbers heretofore unseen.

It is becoming a far more competitive environment. I have now got about six major competitors, whereas it used to be just BT and us. Locally, there is more competition and all of those companies are trying to take on a more global European and worldwide reach. The same thing is being mirrored in Germany, in Holland. They are all needing to expand their business, and that way of expansion is very much going global. It is becoming an increasingly competitive marketplace and it is very difficult.

Sarah Williams,
CEO,
Globecast Northern Europe Ltd

We are basically a domestic business and I think many European businesses have seen themselves as a domestic business. We are now starting to see ourselves not just as a domestic business, but as a global business because our markets have suddenly become global. If we are going to survive, we have to be out in the world in a way that we haven't before.

John Roberts,
CEO,
The Post Office

In fact, the Internet may become the single most-powerful generator of change in European business. The Internet is giving consumers, and even the individual customer, a window of information that looks right inside our companies, and as a consequence eliminates all hiding places for less-than-satisfactory products and services. Everything we do, say, and produce is open for everyone to see, evaluate, and talk about. The veil of secrecy is fast disappearing, and to those not prepared, the open scrutiny of their businesses will be devastating. In fact, as one of the interviewees for this book said, "If the Customer isn't Job 1, there may be no jobs at all!"

The leadership skills necessary to deal effectively with this changing environment—sure to become even more complex, multi-dimensional and speeded up with each passing month—are the focus of this book.

Rather than write a theoretical essay on what I think the problems and solutions might be, my firm conducted over fifty face-to-face interviews with chief executives and senior business leaders of major European corporations—the people on the front lines of 21st century Europe. This book synthesizes the insights these leaders have gained while living and making decisions in today's changing business environment.

THE RESEARCH AND THE COMPANIES

We went to European business leaders—in technology, communications, finance, manufacturing, food, and retail—in hopes of getting a handle on the situation as it is, and as it is likely to evolve in the near and not-so-distant future.

COMPANY	NAME	POSITION	Industry Sector
3i Group plc	Brian Larcombe	President & CEO	Financial Services/Investment
ABN Amro Holding N.V.	Dolf van den Brink	Member of the Board	Banking
Aegon N.V.	Kees Storm	Chairman, Executive Board	Insurance
Arthur Andersen	Jim Wadia	Worldwide Managing Partner	Consultancy
The Axel Johnson Group	Antonia Ax:son Johnson	Chairman	Retail
BAE Systems	Sir Richard Evans	Chairman	Aircraft Manufacturing
Barco N.V.	Hugo Vandamme	President & CEO	Engineering
BBC Worldwide	Rupert Gavin	Chief Executive	Media
Belgacom	John Goossens	President & CEO	Telecoms
BG plc	David Varney	CEO	Utilities/Gas
BG Transco plc	Phil Nolan	CEO	Gas
British Nuclear Fuels plc	John Taylor	Former CEO	Utilities/Nuclear
BT UK	Bill Cockburn	Managing Director	Telecoms
BT plc	Sir Peter Bonfield	Chief Executive	Telecoms
BT plc	John Steele	Group Personnel Director	Telecoms
Carlsberg A/S	Flemming Lindeløv	President & CEO	Brewing
Citibank N.A.	Robert Binney	Managing Director	Banking
Coca-Cola Beverages plc	Neville Isdell	President	Soft Drinks
Connolly Luxury Goods	Simon Merriman	Former Director	Luxury Consumer Goods
CWB Systems Services plc	Christiane Wuillamie	Chairman	IT
Dresdner Kleinwort Benson	Gerd Häusler	Chairman	Banking
The Economist Group	Helen Alexander	CEO	Information Services/Publishing
EDS	David Thorpe	Vice President Global Operations Information Solutions	Information Services
Egmont International Holding A/S	Jan Froeshaug	Group President and CEO	Information Services/Publishing
Electrocomponents plc	Robert Lawson	CEO	Electronics
Electrolux	Michael Treschow	President & CEO	Household Durables/ White Goods
Energis plc	Michael Grabiner	CEO	Telecoms
Ford of Europe Inc.	Nicholas Scheele	Chairman	Auto
Frito-Lay Europe	Bill McLaughlin	Former President & CEO	Food/Beverage
Frito-Lay Europe	Dale Gallagher	VP Operations	Food/Beverage
Frito-Lay Southern Europe	Marco Jesi	President	Food/Beverage
Frito-Lay Europe, Africa, Md East	Tim Pulido	Regional VP Sales & Marketing	Food/Beverage

COMPANY	NAME	POSITION	Industry Sector
Global One	Gary Forsee	Former CEO	Telecoms
Globecast Northern Europe Ltd	Sarah Williams	CEO	Information Services/Media
Goldman Sachs International	Peter Sutherland	Chairman & MD	Financial Services
Granada Group plc	Charles Allen	CEO	Information Services/Media
International Paper Europe S.A.	Robert Amen	President	Paper/Packaging
Interdan A/S	Vagn Holck Andersen	Chairman	
Liverpool City Council	David Henshaw	CEO,	Public Service
Lobo n.v.	Lode Beckers	Chairman	Financial Services
McDonald's UK	Paul Preston	Chairman	Food/Beverasge
National Power plc	Keith Henry	Former CEO	UT/Electricity
Nortel Networks	Gary Donahee	President Service Provider Sales-Americas	Telecoms
Pepsi Cola International	Malcolm Hall	Chief Financial Officer	Food/Beverage
The Post Office	John Roberts	CEO	Government/Postal Service
Premier Oil plc	Charles Jamieson	CEO	Oil
Stephen Raby Associates	Stephen Raby	Managing Director	Recruitment
Reed Elsevier	Nigel Stapleton	Former Joint Chairman & CEO	Information Services/Publishing
Reuters plc	Peter Job	CEO	Information Services/Media
Scottish & Newcastle plc	Brian Stewart	Chief Executive	Brewing
SE Banken Group	Jacob Wallenberg	Chairman	Financial Services
Societe Generale de Belgique	Christine Morin Postel	Chief Executive	Financial Services
Solvay S.A.	Baron Daniel Janssen	Chairman	Chemicals
Spray Razorfish	Per Bystedt	Chairman	IT
St. Paul International Insurance Company Limited	Mark Pabst	President & COO	Insurance
Svenska Handelsbanken	Tom Hedelius	Chairman	Banking
Total Fina S.A.	Thierry Desmarest	Chairman & CEO	Oil Exploration
UCB S.A.	Georges Jacobs	Chairman, Executive Committee	Pharmaceuticals
Van Leer Packaging	Willem de Vlugt	Former Chairman & CEO	Paper/Packaging
Vickers plc	Baron Paul Buysse	CEO	Engineering
Volvo AB	Leif Johansson	President & CEO	Auto
Walkers Snack Foods	Martin Glenn	President & CEO	Food/Beverage
Waste Management Intl.	Bo Gabrielson	Former CEO	UT/Waste

Things change; you have to be alert all the time. No long-term plans. You have to be very flexible.

Tom Hedelius,
Chairman,
Svenska Handelsbanken

Equipped with a standard set of questions, yet committed to keeping the dialogue light and conversational, we were able to probe beneath the companies' "official story"—the facts and figures—to the beliefs, hopes, concerns, and even the fears of the people who run those companies. What emerged from these dialogues? A set of powerful ideas on how leadership skills must change to better match the needs of the European marketplace of the 21st century. Recognizable patterns have already begun to appear on the radar screen of European business. They may be slightly out of focus, but you see them each time you scan the horizon. You can't quite identify them—they are just blurry blips—but every time you look at the screen, they're slightly closer and a little bit bigger.

Talking with a variety of people involved in this business climate has allowed us to sharpen the picture; to focus a telescope on these radar blips. The interviews have given us a wider field of vision into the phenomena that will be so critical to us all in the coming years.

This book contains what I like to call a few "big ideas". Not every one of them will turn out exactly as described in these pages, since the tapestry of 21st century European business is still being woven. Yet no matter its final design, the five key-principles featured in this book are worthy of consideration *now* by all those truly interested in business success and effective leadership. It has been said, "the mind, once stretched with a new idea, can never go back to its original shape." I hope the ideas in this book will stretch your mind, challenge old assumptions, and encourage you to try out some new skills, to grow a little, to learn. If this book causes you to think, and maybe to *rethink* a few things, then the effort will have been a success.

HOW WILL THE WORLD OF WORK BE DIFFERENT IN 21ST CENTURY EUROPE?

External forces and multiple factors, any one of which would throw most companies off-kilter, are already compelling businesses to behave differently. Computing power continues to expand, forcing us to re-evaluate how we manage information.

The global marketplace is becoming wide-open and highly competitive. Already the U.S., Asia and Latin America compete to bring goods and services to our customers whose loyalties, let's face it, are easily swayed. The drive for greater cost-reduction, increased scale, and broadened scope of products and services is forcing consolidation across industries. Daily mergers, acquisitions, and mega-mergers are profoundly altering the business landscape in Europe. While telecommunications will likely be the industry most dramatically changed over the next two to five years, major changes are also affecting such sectors as

I think the fundamental challenges for Europe are firstly, that it doesn't become a Fortress Europe. Secondly, that we do not allow our cost base to be regulated to the highest level, so that everything is levelled up rather than levelled to what it should be. The third challenge is going to be equalising education. I think the whole area of education is too disparate.

Bob Lawson,
CEO,
Electrocomponents plc

> From the market perspective, barriers will be falling in Europe as it becomes more and more one big market, despite the different cultural backgrounds. I think the Euro and the new technology will help to accelerate that process. If you take it from a competitive, legislative and technological point of view, I think the key word is "change", and a faster pace of change.
>
> *John Goossens,*
> *President & CEO,*
> *Belgacom*

supermarkets and financial services, not to mention aerospace, manufacturing, energy exploration and other industries.

As countries privatise and deregulate industries, once-sovereign cultures become open to outside competition. The telephone industry will see new licenses within countries where historically, the order of the realm was the monopolistic entity. Needless to say, this change has spawned hundreds of competitors; two hundred of these so-called "alternate operators" have emerged in the United Kingdom alone, and their numbers throughout Europe increase at the rate of about one per day. Traditional outfits like British Telecom, Deutsche Telekom, and France Telecom have their work cut out for them competing against new providers of goods and services offered at significantly reduced prices. What's more, a single European currency will make prices more transparent across the board. Barriers to entry into many, many businesses are dropping. At the same time, technology continues to speed up business under the mantle of the Internet. Freer and more unpredictable competition arises from this technology as competitors, once excluded, now enjoy access to our traditional customers.

Business leaders today face whole new sets of situations every day: new and more complex boards and government bodies to grapple with; multiple markets and more competitors than ever; multi-cultural stakeholders; employees who live in different countries and speak multiple languages. Much of the business landscape these leaders traverse looks nothing like the one in which they learned their business skills. Small wonder so many business people feel the ground is shifting under their feet.

The crux of the matter is that all these changes—forces, really—are happening simultaneously. Today's chief executive must face challenges from all directions—just like in the ten-year-old's computer game—handling multiple levels of risk, all at once.

OUT OF THE FORTRESS —INTO THE FRAY

Successful companies will recognise that *Fortress Europe* of protectionism won't be able to sustain itself; protectionism no longer works. Successful companies must become global, internationally competitive companies. Some companies have gotten there already, but many have not. As the national barriers truly come down, the *attitudinal Fortress mindset* has to crumble as well. To be globally competitive, business can't hide behind the tariff wall or indulge in the old habits of past business practices.

Competitive pressures will only intensify as the European Union becomes more and more of

You are going to have CEOs who are trying to encourage their staff, or their immediate cohorts, and other people in the organisation, to remember that they are part of a bigger organisation, so they can't just live in a silo. They've got to think about the impact of decisions they make on others. I really think we are going to be looking for people to be self-starters, use their initiative, and be innovative. Because everything is happening so much faster now. And it's going to increase in pace. So we are going to need executives who are prepared to take risks. The message today from the top is "take risks."

John Steele,
Group Personnel Director,
BT plc

Directionally, Europe has come together as an entity. As monetary union progresses, a greater degree of political union must follow. Some of the sovereignty of the member states will go. I am not sure that this will lead to an open European market, but to a redrawing of sectors in the European market. The sectorisation of the market will not be along national borders.

Phil Nolan,
CEO,
BG Transco plc

an open market where not only prices, but practices, are transparent. A French business cannot survive catering only to the French market; a German network will no longer work as such. Both will need to be a pan-European or even international network.

For some countries, political challenges might be greater than those griping businesses. This will be especially true for the smaller or traditionally more isolated states. Sweden, for example, until recently had created a figurative wall behind a welfare state; where powerful taxation policies and unique environmental and labour laws were the rule. With the EU and the pressure for global competition, Sweden is suddenly part of 21st century Europe, and the burden is on Swedish politicians to align with the rest of Europe. If they do not, one CEO in our study has predicted, some large companies may relocate their head offices to another country.

Here is what we know for sure: Europe can no longer survive as a group of separate entities battened against each other and the rest of the world. Many leaders already acknowledge the coming changes and agree that businesses are moving away from *Fortress Europe* and towards *Global Europe*. For one thing, Europe is not big enough to trade only amongst its own countries. Europe is a big market, to be sure, but there is an even bigger one nipping at its heels. Unless Europe can become globally competitive, it will be priced and produced out of the global marketplace.

THE SLOW DANCE IS OVER, GET YOUR BOOGIE SHOES ON!

"I'll sit this one out", or "I'll wait and see", as responses to the changing economic movement, are cop-outs that just won't work anymore. In 1996, we listened to a speech by Douglas Hurd, Britain's former foreign secretary, about the coming European Union. When pressed by a member of the audience to define Britain's stand on the EU, and particularly the adoption of the Euro, Hurd resorted to political babble and even suggested that Britain should simply "wait and see"! Now, at the beginning of the new millennium, Britain is scrambling to regain influence in the European Union. The tidal wave is coming. Do you want to be a surfer taking advantage of the moving forces, or a victim of a tsunami? Unprepared companies won't know what hit them. Competitors will creep out of the woodwork, providing equally good, more diverse products at lower cost.

It's survival time, and it's a time for leadership!

European companies have to get out into the global environment in a major way, and at the

Swedish executives are extremely international considering the size and peripheral location of Sweden. I am probably much more international than the average American executive. On the other hand, the United States is a rich and big continent, whereas Sweden is a small country on the outskirts of Europe. I do think it has benefited me, because the globalisation that people are talking about and the openness with which information flows in stocks, shares and currencies to pop music, art and literature, has been a way of life ever since I was very young.

Antonia Ax:son Johnson,
Chairman,
The Axel Johnson Group

Soon there will be globalisation of the capital markets and you start getting
companies that have to
be sensitive to ROI who
have never been sensitive
to ROI. In industries that
have moved from being
family dominated to
being publicly held and
having to create share-
owner value rather than
family wealth, you are
going to see incredible
pressures on profit mar-
gins, both from the share-
owners as well as from
global competitors.

Robert Amen,
President,
International Paper Europe S.A.

same time do business very differently within
Europe in order to cut costs, improve quality, and
reduce the time it takes to get products to market.
To change the ways in which things are done, we
have to fundamentally shift how we do business.
And that is the job of leadership! The change
must come through the leadership process. It
must be led—it can't be mandated. Organisations have to change, people have to change,
cultures have to change. You can't just reorganise and expect everybody to behave differently.
The savvier companies realise that if they must
change in order to survive, then they are going
to have to somehow get people to change inside
the company. And that is the responsibility of
leadership.

A big challenge awaits
leadership in Europe.
There are not many of
what I would call good
leaders. If you look at
Europe broadly and look
at the top CEOs, modern
leadership is just not
there. Going into the 21st
century, the challenge is
how to get the European
companies to adapt.
Time is becoming more
important. There is less
and less time.

Christiane Wuillamie,
Chairman,
CWB Systems Services plc

NEW LEADERSHIP FOR
21ST CENTURY EUROPE

Technology and global communication have
made it necessary for business to step up the
pace from miles per hour to *Web speed.* Technology has not only fueled the entry of competition into European business, it has also given
the customer a more integral role in driving
business. The old model was simply that you
delivered a product or service to a customer
and that was it. Now, customers are becoming
more sophisticated every day and, as a result,

seeking new ways to get the same or better products faster and cheaper—and our competition is only too happy to accommodate. The focus of management must become much more centred on the customer. "How do we get them to stay loyal and to spend more?" will be our guiding question.

In a fast-paced global economy, too much happens that needs too much attention for one leader to do it all. The archetype of the self-contained, lone commander no longer works. When the former Director General of the BBC, Sir John Birt, stepped down, the search for a replacement led to a discussion aimed less at *who* should fill the position than *how* it should be filled. Some felt the job required more skill and focus than one person could supply. The realisation hit home that the job of managing both the talent and business arenas was too big for one person: to successfully run the BBC in the 21st century would take an effective team.

And so it is with all of European business. The key role of the CEO in the new environment will be team builder and team motivator. The model for corporate structure will be not rigid hierarchy, but "distributed leadership".

Management teams in the future will involve more players than one or two individuals and the office of the chairman. A "dream team" is really what we are talking about. In order to create a "dream team" to run the organisation,

The real challenge for business leaders in the new Europe will be to think European rather than nationally. This is compounded by the other big issues of competition, technology, deregulation, and the very speed of change. Leadership will definitely be more difficult in the coming decade!

*Sir Peter Bonfield,
Chief Executive,
BT plc*

I think there are going to be dramatic changes in the way companies equip themselves, in the profile of the people they employ, in the technical skills of the people they employ, and in the way they are structured. So you can pick whatever domain; for example, teleworking is a concept that is going to happen more and more. Everything will be changing except it will be changing faster.

*John Goossens,
President & CEO,
Belgacom*

First of all, there has to be a greater understanding of the cultural diversity in each of those countries. That's not to make excuses for it, but it's to understand it and then deal with it. Understanding how to manage across those boundaries, across those languages, across those cultures, how to avoid the "one size fits all," but at the same time not to give up the prize of leverage, common process, and common approach—that's a big challenge for the CEO.

David Thorpe,
Vice President Global Operations
Information Solutions,
EDS

individuals must align with each other, and the organisation must align with the customer.

HERE IS SOME HELP

This book offers two kinds of help. One is for the company itself; the principles and ideas that can be used to build organisational effectiveness in 21st century Europe. The other is for the people who run the companies; tools for personal effectiveness. Because the way the business game is played internally is not cutting it any better than the way the game is going externally. Employees are becoming more and more frustrated with work environments that cannot keep up with the changes occurring in the marketplace, that therefore are not offering the rewards and satisfaction they need. And unlike our story of the executive and his son's computer game at the beginning of this chapter, there is no "slow speed" on the desk of today's European business leaders. It's definitely a time for leadership!

1 The Emerging European Landscape

Europe, via the EU, has taken a long forty years to evolve into the race-paced, technologically astute, competitive and wide-open marketplace it is today. The context in which companies have to survive now is anything but the slow, protected Fortress Europe environment of the past. Bureaucratic structures that once sustained and defended national companies are disappearing. Now, aided by the speed of the Internet, the rapid evolution of the European business environment may best be measured not in quarterly reportings and traditional business years, but in "Web speed"—and internet years.

Increasing global competition, mergers, privatisation, new labour legislation, ongoing technological changes, and a savvy consumer population have levelled the playing field for European business. Business leaders must be able to respond quickly. They must adopt principles to

The EU and the open market obviously open up huge opportunities for the efficiently run, well-managed, well-distributed organisation that is able to take product to market at a competitive price. And, similarly, it blows away the localised operator that was being preserved in some way by protectionism. Running these companies is going to be a very, very complex task because you are going to have to understand the diversity of consumer needs.

Rupert Gavin,
Chief Executive,
BBC Worldwide

If I can talk about a worry or concern, it is the potential increase in central government restrictions from Brussels or Strasbourg. Obviously, Europe has to be competitive against other regions of the world. Social legislation is a very easy or obvious example. If we're putting too much cost base on our own organisations within the European community, it is very difficult for them to compete against some of the Asian economies, for example, or China when that comes through.
So central government restrictions could be a big factor in the way that Europe will be changing, and obviously as Europe harmonizes more and more, that is likely to become stronger and stronger.

Stephen Raby,
Managing Director,
Stephen Raby Associates

help their organisations, and their employees, change the way they work and the way they treat customers to succeed in the emerging business landscape. We are not talking about management fads, tricks, or recycled theories. We are talking about effective leadership principles to activate effective behaviours. To face the fundamental external changes afoot—happening at lightning speed, to boot—we need the leverage and understanding fundamental principles provide in order to be effective.

In the marketplace of the previous decade, whenever we came to a crossroads we saw two or three paths to choose from. Now, the crossroads looks more like a spaghetti tangle, with routes going in every direction. Each path is an opportunity to be travelled, or at least explored, quickly. There is no time for an elabourate five-year planning process. In many cases, we don't even have five months.

But just because world markets have gone grand prix doesn't mean we must do everything at a frenzied speed. Doing business as usual, only faster, is a design to fail. One of the CEOs we interviewed reminded us of one definition of insanity: "doing the same thing over and over, or doing it faster and faster, and expecting a different result"! We need forward vision to successfully navigate in this speeded-up world. We can't drive a car at autobahn speeds using only the rear-view mirror. We have to use every field of vision available. To move ahead in this new speeded up environment, we need an effective set of leadership principles, not just the same old skills done faster.

NEW PRINCIPLES CAN ACTIVATE NEW BEHAVIOURS

Understanding and applying the principle of gravity helped the Wright brothers get off the ground and helped mankind get to the moon and back. This principle of physical science is at play whether we wish it to be or not, or are aware of it or not. A principle is a fundamental truth that helps solve problems and can take us to a new level of understanding. Principles are at work no matter the circumstances, no matter whether you believe in them or not.

That microscopic bacteria are linked to disease is a fundamental principle that has shaped and reshaped human cultures for centuries. Yet, in the Middle Ages people assumed that disease was caused by demons that projected alien spirits into their victims. Folks also thought that fresh meat spoiled because a sick person gazed upon it. These are theories, or at best, beliefs that help to answer the question of why things are the way they are. But while they may provide an explanation, and people may even believe them, they are not principles that lead to greater understanding and a capacity to control our destiny. Theories and

I think inevitably the CEO has become a more strategic role. Historically, there was confusion as to whether the CEO was the Chief Operating Officer. The CEO is going to have a more strategic perspective than he would have had ten years ago. He must spend more time on strategy and strategy evolution than being the hands-on Chief Executive people were looking for in the past.

Brian Stewart,
Chief Executive,
Scottish & Newcastle plc

beliefs don't get results, they just give comfort.

We now know that spoiled meat is a phenomenon governed by the bacteria principle. No matter what the people of an earlier time *believed*, the basic principle that microscopic bacteria caused disease and spoiled meat was sound. Once this principle was understood, its application led to entire industries built around health care, pharmaceuticals, and food safety and preservation—and saved millions of lives around the globe.

Similarly, in the business world, we are encountering uncharted environments requiring us to better understand fundamental principles. And, since understanding drives behaviours, it is important to develop a deeper understanding of the fundamental principles of leadership in complex and fast-moving business environments. With a deeper understanding of leadership principles, we can activate new behaviours to move our companies forward.

BUSINESS PRINCIPLES THAT SHAPED THE PAST MAY NOT FIT FOR TOMORROW...

This book is titled *A Time for Leadership*. It is not *A Time for Financial Engineers*; it is not *A Time for Technologists*. Those folks are well into doing what they do. What business leaders need to address is *how* companies are led. Why? Firstly,

> Tomorrow's chief executive will have to get used to, in case he isn't already, the fact that we operate in a wider and more open economic area called Europe or the European Single Market. And we all are better off if we feel confident with that. The more we understand and are enthusiastic about this new given, the easier it will be to adapt and live with the remaining cultural and other differences. We should pay more attention than ever before to what makes us European. We still think differently, eat differently, talk different languages. So there is going to be a greater need for an awareness of what we have in common regardless of the remaining differences. That deeper awareness should be reflected in the way business is conducted in Europe.
>
> *Lode Beckers,*
> *Chairman,*
> *Lobo n.v.*

On one level, Europe is becoming an entity with the European Union. But in other terms, it's becoming a series of sub-regions. We are seeing more and more regional business plans rather than country by country business plans.

David Henshaw,
CEO,
Liverpool City Council

I think the biggest change we are going to have to make in Europe is to learn how to accept failure. We are too risk-averse, we don't accept failure easily, and we are not flexible enough.

Jim Wadia,
Worldwide Managing Partner,
Arthur Andersen

subsidies, a captive customer base, and a captive work force. The dependency on Authority Power as the primary leadership model produced a strong leader and a centralised autocratic organisation. The leader was the one who knew the most; the leader had all the information—after all, the top was the only place all the data ever converged. He (or more infrequently she) had the most experience; he was older, more mature. He had deep connections to those in power. Everyone deferred to him. And he had total control of the board.

In today's global marketplace, where there is a fast flow of capital, goods, and labour, and where labour and consumers speak different languages and value different traditions, the old style of authoritarian leadership simply doesn't apply. In the same way that we know the principle of bacteria and disease does not apply in the cold vacuum of outer space, so too, the autocratic principles of the past fall flat in the New European environment.

We need a model that offers a lot more leverage. So much new information travels via the Internet, at blitzen speed, no one person can access or process it all effectively. When this information plastering is combined with the rapid influx of new competitors, the cultural diversity of the consumer base, and the multinational labour force, it becomes clear that it is physically impossible for any one human being to be sensitive enough to develop, let alone dictate, successful business strategies.

IT'S A NEW EUROPEAN LANDSCAPE!

To be clear, Europe *looks* the same as it has for decades. There are still distinct cultures separated by traditional geographic borders, different languages spoken, and nationalistic ties and interests. It is how Europe *feels* that is changing; how it feels to the businessperson, and most importantly, to the consumer.

A dynamic European ambition has begun to reshape Europe into an effective local and global competitor. The changes in business practice are happening faster than local politics can keep up. So, when we talk the talk of business—relocating, investing, hiring labour, the flow of goods and capital, the need for pan-European supply chains—boundaries have less and less relevance.

The new ambitious Europe regards itself more as a set of regions rather than a group of separate nations. Strategies are beginning to develop around critical regional boundaries, not national. For example, Frito-Lay Europe adapts its business and marketing strategy to particular major European regions: UK (United Kingdom); SEBU (Southern Europe Business Unit); NEBU (Northern Europe Business Unit); AMEA (Africa, Middle East); and EEBU (Eastern

Europe will have to be careful. She could put herself in the position where she is uncompetitive. There is no question that the single greatest factor in influencing people's purchase decisions, in my opinion, is value for money. They are going to go where they get, in their minds, the greatest value for money. If Europe, for all of its goodness, is seen to be not good value in relation to what people can purchase from other places in the world, then she is going to have trouble.

Paul Preston,
Chairman,
McDonald's UK

Europe Business Unit), roughly following customer taste preferences as well as similar purchas-
ing habits. Within Great Britain, a relatively small
geographic marketplace, Northwest England is
seen as a region. Even though there is still a cen-
tralist government in the UK and labour laws in
place, more and more, regions from one country
make deals with a region from another, creating
strategic alliances to produce goods. And they
tend to bypass the traditional channels of central
government. This phenomenon has produced a
heightened awareness of regional differences and
regional powers. Clearly, the need to accept differences will only become more important as
Europe enters the global market.

THE ECONOMIC EUROPEAN UNION: NEW FREEDOM, NEW DEMANDS

To survive in the new European market, businesses will have to be innovative. They will have
to develop flexibility, still a strange concept in
Europe, not one we associate with the Fortress.
Too bad: European business must learn to take
risks, absorb failure, and bounce back. Business
in the United States is much more risk-oriented,
as it is in Asia. Failure is part of the scenario.
Two years after a business fails, it comes back,
reorganised, to try again. Among Europeans,
failure is historically taken more seriously.

There is no magic way into the future of the EU, but most agree that succeeding in Europe will come down to fighting for the hearts and minds of customers, which also goes against the grain of tradition in Europe. Most large companies have evolved within a sphere of influence. They have communities of interest, and a whole series of complex cross-trading relationships. They have effectively protected these markets; whether they're linked into the Old Establishment, whether they're in Germany where they're linked into the banks, or whether they're in Italy and linked into the families. Those closely held markets will no longer be sustainable. Customer loyalty needs to be earned on an almost daily basis.

The flood of superior goods and services from outside Europe will test and most likely break that loyalty. In order to survive in the new Europe, corporations have to change fundamental mindsets and values. European companies will have to move away from managing long-standing strategic relationships, to focusing on both the European and global consumer base, continually asking: "What do the customers want?"; "How good are the products and services we provide?"; "How can we make them better, at less cost?"; "Where can we gain added-value to improve our profit margins?"

Along with these pressing demands, the EU has brought crucial competitive aspects into

Communication is not a one-way process; it's a two-way process, and unless you can have a two-way communication, you are really going to miss a trick if you think that the technology is a substitute for the interaction.

Nicholas Scheele,
Chairman,
Ford of Europe Inc.

focus. One is the urgent need for a new level of competency. Companies are scrambling to come up with new efficient strategies because the huge economic market sorely challenges their old ones. The EU now offers tremendous opportunities for well-managed organisations to take products to market at competitive prices in huge quantities. And it destroys the local operation that was being preserved in some way by protectionism.

The EU has also brought into focus a new local culture consciousness. Cultural rootedness is enormously powerful. And it will be that way for a very long period of time. In the U.S., marketers have known for some time that great opportunities exist in business addressing African American and Hispanic communities, as well as those of other ethnic groups living in the U.S. European business has to come to the same understanding. We must find a way to speak to, manage, and motivate people from different cultures who value different types of products and services.

There is no cultural unity in Europe—only diversity. And opportunity. Whereas an American marketing executive might not have to think about different motivational structures for Denver and San Diego, the European executive must examine and address the differences between a customer in Southern Italy and another in Northern Wales.

The third aspect that's coming into focus, although still a little blurry, is the role of regula-

I think there are three things that are happening that are vital to any business in Europe. The first is a phenomenal change in information technology; the ability to communicate and make an impact without the barrier of space and time. The second change driver is the single market: globalisation. Europeans don't have a global mentality like in the States. Nothing is big here. And the third one is deregulation; because of cross-country competition, because of harmonization. And this is bringing a lot of complexity and a lot of discontinuity in the way we do business, and in the way we operate.

Marco Jesi,
President,
Frito-Lay Southern Europe

tion within the EU. There is, after all, a love of bureaucracy in Old Europe. You can take Europe out of the Fortress but can you take the Fortress out of Europe? The New Europe brings with it some Old World protectionist tendencies, and these tendencies may actualise into regulatory cement.

TECHNOLOGY:
THE UPSIDE—THE DOWNSIDE

Computer-driven communication has accelerated business in Europe just as much as in the United States. Much more is done over the Internet in a few minutes than was once accomplished in hours of presentations, conferences, and meetings. The rapid, easy flow of information widely shared among players has become one of the invisible assets of any company.

Technology is a double-edged sword in terms of relationships and communications. I hear people say all the time, "I just can't keep up with my e-mail." This technology is supposed to help us stay close and to stay on top of things, but in a sense, it has caused an avalanche. It is also depersonalising relationships. The very thing we thought would help us build relationships across boundaries actually can become what weakens them. Human beings need human connections. We need lively rapport and an opportunity to

The closer integration of various national European economies has meant that national companies are becoming European companies; the speed of this evolution will vary from industry to industry. What we will see in the future are businesses with a European character rather than a national one. At Dresdner Bank, for example, we define our core market as "Euroland" and not just Germany.

Gerd Häusler,
Chairman,
Dresdner Kleinwort Benson

develop that rapport. Trust and rapport create the glue essential to effective business and competitive advantage.

MOST OF US ARE OVERWHELMED

You must have more devolved responsibility to be able to respond to the demands of the customer.

Sir Peter Bonfield,
Chief Executive,
BT plc

Many European companies are struggling to remain competitive in the tidal wave of change that the single market, deregulation, and globalisation have brought about. This drive toward global effectiveness is causing great stress. Many are looking within the organisation to the leadership for guidance. Their instincts are good: The key for thriving into the next century lies with leadership. It will take some very savvy leaders and aligned executive teams to successfully take European business out of its protected Fortress and into a global and international network.

SO LET'S SUM IT UP:
WHAT WE THINK WE KNOW,
AND KNOW WE DON'T... SO FAR

❖ When we get monetary union, a fair degree of political union must follow.
❖ Some of the economic sovereignty of the states will go. Whether this will lead to an open European market is uncertain,

moving companies from success in an old environment to success in the new is a leadership responsibility. How to get there from here is the issue of leadership—"there" being equipped to deal with new governments and government bodies, multiple new markets, competitors and investors, and multiple national locations. And we can't homogenize Europe. Who would want to? The European Union in not the United States of Europe! It is a complex set of histories, cultures, markets, and customers. What will happen to the European tapestry over the next five to ten years is unique. We must approach it with leadership that is appropriate for the time and the place. We must develop unifying principles that galvanize and transcend the differences in the workforce and the marketplace. Europe is full of diversity. A pan-European company must develop a similar diversity to survive.

Secondly, we need to address how companies are led because organisations tend to be shadows of their leaders. They bear the imprint of those at the helm. If anything new and different is going to happen, it is going to happen because leadership works in a new and different way. It will be the leadership that sets the new standards of work behaviour, values, and customer service.

The style of business leadership within Fortress Europe was developed over hundreds of years on a country-by-country basis and in a marketplace characterised by heavy monopolies,

Leaders in the new Europe are going to need to think from a production perspective or an efficiency perspective beyond national boundaries. Any company that delivers a service or makes a physical thing is going to have to think, "What is the minimum efficient scale I need?" They are going to have to get out of the old thinking of defining immediately a market area as synonymous to a country area. That is not necessarily the best way to go, and that actually does involve some pretty major changes in thinking.

Martin Glenn,
President & CEO,
Walkers Snack Foods

but it will certainly lead to a redrawing of sectors in the European market. The sectorization of the market will follow regional, not national, lines.

❖ We will see free movement of capital. There will be free movement of goods as well as labour to a point.

❖ Even though national boundaries will no longer correspond to business boundaries, that does not mean that Europe will be *boundaryless*. Most leaders agree that Europe is too political to be boundaryless.

❖ More likely, we will see degrees of sovereignty.

❖ The abolition of exchange controls and the free movement of capital will certainly evolve, as will monetary instruments that no longer belong to the states. Some states will exercise more control than others. We may not get a total market.

❖ What shakes out may look like some sort of *Federation of European States*, but that is as far as it will get. There will be some state barriers. But capital—human, intellectual and monetary—will be shared.

❖ There will be transparency of pricing. Even in the U.S., there are still local taxes, and local taxes affect pricing. What government can subsist without tax-raising powers? The markets will hold imperfections due to taxation.

As the national barriers have truly come down, then the Fortress Europe barriers have got to come down, because to be globally competitive, you can't shelter behind the tariff wall. We've all seen what happens if you have tariff walls— you do not sustain competitiveness.

Nicholas Scheele,
Chairman,
Ford of Europe Inc.

You have to realise Europe will change with the EU. There will be transparency all over Europe in prices, and I think the Euro will mean a strong integration, stronger than we can imagine. There will still be cultural differences and there will be sub-cultures. But there will be more and more harmonisation in the social welfare aspect; in people's thinking. So therefore I think that you can feel that you are a Dane, you can feel that you are a German, but you have to *think* that you are a European.

Vagn Holck Andersen,
Chairman,
Interdan A/S

I think there is another very key pressure in Europe, which is the enlargement of Europe towards the East.

John Taylor,
Former CEO,
British Nuclear Fuels plc

❖ Companies are going to have to internationalise staff, taking into account regional variations.

❖ The legal framework for commerce and politics will be fascinating. The philosophy of law is different all around Europe, and harmonizing specific laws will be a major challenge. What will be the common denominator?

❖ Will competition law be the same in all European states? If not, the situation will likely give rise to some irksome anomalies.

❖ The legal system will likely develop tax systems that will be tacked on; it's unlikely we'll see a complete redesign of sovereign legal systems.

❖ How will the legal systems in independent countries develop, given that market sectors will be redrawn, and not on national boundaries?

❖ Where is the jurisdiction of a transaction done on *e-commerce*; the location of the seller?—the location of the buyer? How do you collect such a tax? How will *e-commerce* cover the movement from direct taxation to indirect taxation? Should there be no tax at all on the transaction?

❖ Companies must affect the total reorganisation of ideas, values, and efficiencies in order to play the game in the New Europe.

Operating effectively in a world ready and willing to eliminate those who can't adapt requires learning how to navigate the twists and turns, and having the intestinal fortitude to face and negotiate the risks. Becoming grounded in the leadership principles to be covered in the following chapters will enhance your capability, because the last thing any business wants to see flash on the screen before them is "GAME OVER!"

I am president of a body called the European Foundation of Quality Management, and as a result, I chair a Board of Governors which consists of thirteen European CEOs. The thing that fascinates me is that their businesses now, whether they are based in Belgium, Germany, France, wherever, are nearly all multinational and some of them are becoming global. Europe of the 20th century, perhaps conditioned by war, has always been inward-focused, looking maybe just across the border to next door. I think some of that happened in business as well, that people were always looking at the competitor as being the person only nearest to the border post. Whereas, I think what is happening now and what will happen in the 21st century, also driven by telecommunications, IT systems, is that Europe will see itself as part of the world in a way that maybe it hasn't before .

John Roberts,
CEO,
The Post Office

2 New Principles for Leadership in 21st Century Europe

GUIDING PRINCIPLES FOR SUCCESSFUL LEADERSHIP

Drawing on the interviews done specifically for this book, as well as on more than twenty years experience in consulting with the world's leading companies, we have identified ways in which a number of companies are already reorganising to negotiate the seismic changes brought on by the EU. We have synthesized our discoveries into five Guiding Principles of Leadership.

DISTRIBUTED LEADERSHIP

First, leadership in a rapidly changing, complex business environment is a huge job, too complex for a single leader. We need "Distributed Leadership", or "Distributed Wisdom", as I like

I am a believer in dialogue and consensus between the chief executive and the senior management within the organisation. I think that the active involvement of dialogue is time well spent if it helps to create an alignment of view as to where, and in what direction, the company should go. It is something I consciously work on all the time, and it is absolutely an essential element in the culture of both BP and Goldman Sachs, both which I am associated.

Peter Sutherland,
Chairman & MD,
Goldman Sachs International

The concept of "Distributed Leadership" will keep you in touch with the environment. If you want to prepare people for this environment, you have to get leadership further down the organisation. We generally tend to drive managing down the organisation, but not leadership. As an organisation, we have to prepare for acts of leadership further down the organisation. I think that that is the hardest thing for us to do as people sitting at the top. It feels almost like an unnatural act.

Phil Nolan,
CEO,
BG Transco plc

to call it. That means that the role of the CEO is one of influence, not control: the leader is an agent of change, not the sole source of wisdom or decisions.

We also have to prepare more people for bigger leadership roles at all levels of the company. For example, we have found that in a merger or acquisition, country-specific teams that share the same vision and values as the leadership team move more quickly and sensitively within diverse cultures to market the business. They can cut through obstacles with sensitivity to local culture because they are taking into account that the Spanish are different from the Germans and that consumer issues in northern Italy will be different from those in northern Wales.

With markets expanding into different areas and sometimes with only subtle differences in local buying patterns, it would take the chief executive all his waking hours to travel to all the markets and understand all the factors for success. Increasingly, companies are assembling teams of leaders not only to gather information, but to implement company strategies at the local level. Over time, leadership teams make bigger and bigger decisions. To make these business decisions wisely, these leaders must not only understand the values and strategies of the overall firm, but also bear the trust of the chief executive and the board. Distributed Leadership is about shared accountability, which depends on a deterrent to the changes necessary for survival in the complex business environment of 21st century Europe.

Brand and Culture Must Match

We keep our promises on our commitments. We do business ethically. We do more than talk about it; we actually have business processes built around it. We have developed a brand equity. It's an expression of the culture.

Mark Pabst,
President & COO,
St. Paul International Insurance
Company Limited

The third Principle asserts "Brand and Culture Must Match." Until recently, brand image and development was handled in the PR and marketing departments only. This work focused on building consumer expectations, a sort of Pavlovian experiment on the potential customer. We see McDonald's golden arches and desire a hamburger and fries because we have expectations of value, quality, speed of service, and cleanliness that have been ingrained by decades of brand-building activities.

Brand value resides on the balance sheet of today's global competitors. But when brand and culture don't match, the customer experiences cognitive dissonance and perceives the company as lacking integrity and not in alignment with its advertising. In that case, what the company's culture delivers does not support what the brand image promises. A study of British Airways and Virgin Airlines provides a crucible for what happens when brand and culture match, as well as when they do not.

Shadow of the Leader

Organisations are shadows of their leaders. The fourth Principle to emerge from years of consulting and recent European research concerns itself with the preeminence of the leader— and the leadership team—in affecting the behaviour of the entire company. The "Cast of Influence" begins at the top and is both mirrored and magnified all the way to the bottom. The critical corollary that arises from this principle is that performance cannot be mandated; it must be led. And leading, more often than not, involves motivating. It doesn't mean that the CEO has to know and be all things. The task before him might be even harder than that—the leader has to get his or her highly focused, aggressive senior managers to work together and to adopt the attitudes the CEO and/or executive committee envision for the company as a whole, and the goals they want to achieve.

I see the CEO job as not being in this office, but being out in the company. And the moment you go out through the door, then people will look at you and see whether you are living the values of the company. Leaders cast a shadow by their behaviour.

John Roberts,
CEO,
The Post Office

Balance of Life

Finally, the fifth Principle may be what saves the leader from himself. It's called, "Balance of Life". Racing to keep up with daily demands while burning-out our clutches to eke out a slight advantage, has not worked—and won't. We need to adapt to the new demands of an accelerated world in more realistic ways. While

> We are only on this world once, and since I've got family and friends, it's important to enjoy them. I can tell you when my holidays are booked for next year. And unless it's an absolute emergency, I will take the holiday.
>
> *John Taylor,*
> *Former CEO,*
> *British Nuclear Fuels plc*

speed-to-market may be the answer to new product introductions, racing at warp speed is neither the way to make effective business decisions nor the best approach to plotting competitive strategy. To be more effective in a highly complex and fast-moving business world, leaders must actually slow down! When they do, they gain a healthy perspective on business issues and make better quality decisions. And the best way to slow down is to practice a balanced life, spending healthy amounts of time on all valued dimensions of life: family, hobbies, charities, quiet reflection, as well as the world of work.

While this principle may appear to be counterproductive—"How can I afford to slow down when the world is speeding up?"—today's savvy leaders recognise all too well the diminishing returns from too-rapid decision making and rushed thinking. In Chapter Eight we will delve further into this contrary, but highly effective, new business principle.

We will explore these five leadership principles in depth, as well as the solutions they hold for European business leaders. Before we do, however, let us look at some of the strategies upon which we see these principles having the greatest impact.

MERGERS, ACQUISITIONS, AND THE EUROPEAN RUSH FOR SCOPE AND SCALE

One of the most powerful strategies for thriving in an expanding global economy is to obtain scope and scale, and one of the best ways to achieve them is through acquisition. The mergers and acquisitions market in Europe today is creating chaos both exciting and paralysing. The excitement comes from the kind of opportunity we imagine would arise in the merger of, say, Vodaphone with Mannesmann. The magnitude of leverage in the European telecom market boggles the mind.

At the same time, these giga-mergers paralyse because they induce protracted periods of indecision—not to mention indigestion. The merger process focuses all parties on the questions, "Will the merger go through?", "Who is going to win?", and "What is going to happen to me?" Everyone's energies go to the merger and off his or her work. The process, of course, continues for months, if not years. It's deadly in a market as fast as today's. In a millisecond, "GAME OVER!"

For example, the British Telecom/MCI deal went on for a year and a half before it finally died. It cost millions of pounds and stole thousands of people's attention away from the work at hand. The greatest loss was BT's momentum in the marketplace. In the meantime, Energis grew

In terms of a merger, you have got the ego of the individuals coming together and clashing. You have also got the clash of cultures of the two organisations coming together. Certainly the clash of cultures is very *difficult* to manage. You have to re-educate the whole group, not just one group which is the taken-over group. You have to actually re-educate both sides so that both sides perceive one, new combined unit rather than an "us and them" situation. The clash of egos of individuals is always going to happen and a lot of merger activity, to my understanding and experience, has fallen apart on that issue alone.

Stephen Raby,
Managing Director,
Stephen Raby Associates

Merger & acquisition activity will grow a lot in Europe over the next few years, and the nature of those changes, both big mergers and smaller acquisitions, will naturally change the competitive landscape. Europe will consolidate more, and as a result become a more competitive global player.

Brian Larcombe,
President & CEO,
3i Group plc

When we are talking with a company that we may wish to acquire, we always consider closely the cultural issues, and almost always our human resource people are involved in the due diligence process.

Hugo Vandamme,
President & CEO,
Barco N.V.

in market capitalisation, and with Dixon's, helped launch the revolutionary Freeserve Internet service as well; which ultimately influenced the market to such a degree that even BT now has to offer at least one free Internet access service.

In an economic environment such as this one—which demands entry into new cultures, both corporate and social—mergers and acquisitions represent the best strategy. But everything depends on how they are executed. It is extremely hard to put two cultures together so that we get both synergy and savings. And traditional European business executives are not that experienced in creating effective and successful mergers. Most mergers, in fact, fail. That is, they work on the drawing board but not in real life. Just ask anyone what has happened to the brightest of the Bankers Trust crowd following the acquisition by Deutsche Bank: In almost every area, the Bankers Trust people are out and the Deutsche Bank people are in complete control. So much for gaining synergies and creating a global culture able to deal with a global world. It's really a bigger Deutsche Bank.

A legal merger doesn't necessarily make a merging of beliefs, values, and behaviours. The task for us will be to find effective ways of creating mergers and acquisitions across cultural borders that work for employees as well as customers.

PRIVATISATION AND
CREATIVE NEW LEADERSHIP

Privatisation is having a better initial impact than mergers. Privatisation puts decisions in the hands of people who know the business best. This has been a boon to the European marketplace. It has opened it up, ushering in the forces of competition, capitalism, and creative risk-taking. Yet one big problem that can result from privatising and deregulating a major, state-owned business is the creation of an unequal playing field. For example, let's say a new gas company comes in from another country and starts to install gas pipelines. The "outsider" gas company cannot operate at the same level as the incumbent state-owned gas utility can. It's impossible. Phasing-in deregulation to allow competition, on the other hand, levels the playing field more. Technology will aid the transition. It moves so fast, in a few years' time the field may be completely level. Technology will affect privatisation much faster than it happened in America with the break-up of AT&T or the deregulation of the gas utilities.

CHANGE OR DIE

External technological and environmental changes are forcing companies to dance as fast as they can. They are trying to transform

I think when I first joined an industrial company thirty years ago, we regarded our job as communicating what we expected in a very clear way and we checked to make sure it was understood. Today, we want to communicate rather more clearly the aspirations, and we trust the organisation to figure out how those aspirations will be achieved.

David Varney,
CEO,
BG plc

themselves quickly into a new kind of organisation and at the same time protect their core business— what they do best—because that is what they live on. It's a very difficult task, even in stable times.

The problem is, many of today's European companies are doing what they've always done. They are just trying to do it faster. But doing more of the same, only more quickly, is a losing strategy. As Albert Einstein said, "The same level of thinking that caused our problems can't be used to solve them."

Speed is not an abiding principle. Speeding-up old ways is neither effective nor sustainable. It may help in the short run, but eventually it will cause burn-out and the demise of the company. What the new leadership will have to speed-up is its adaptability, on multiple levels.

"Change or Die" has only recently become the battle cry in Europe, born of the effective loss of subsidised workforces, labour regulations, protected regions, and in fact, a whole base of security. An essential role of leadership in this environment is to first recognise that things are changing dramatically, and second, wisely interpret what these changes mean, both to the organisation and to the customer.

Recognising which past tools should be kept and which tossed becomes a tough and critical challenge. How tools need to be modified in order to adapt to the new environment is part of the same consideration. One executive we inter-

I think the successful European organisation will rely a lot on getting people enrolled in plans and strategies. It will be much less of a command-and-control kind of enterprise, and making sure that everybody is brought into some of the strategies and plans is time-consuming; which can be frustrating, but highly fruitful.

Helen Alexander,
CEO,
The Economist Group

real-time sharing of information.

In Chapter Three, we will explore in detail the Principle of Distributed Leadership, with examples and insights from our interviews.

Culture Impacts the Balance Sheet as Well as Productivity

The second principle is that "Culture Impacts Performance". The collective behaviour of employees affects all facets of the company. Without a doubt, the ideas and beliefs held by a group shape company results. If we ignore this fact, we find ourselves back in the old "GAME OVER!" situation.

Corporate culture is not easy to identify, especially for senior management, because they are so much a part of the culture. In essence, employees tend to have "familiarity blindness" when it comes to their own culture. They often see it as the "way things are done", yet few realise that culture is a collection of beliefs about the company and about work, some of which get in the way of superior performance. While everyone acknowledges that social cultures are distinct and influence the way a particular country or society interacts with the world, few chief executives have the same insight into their own corporate culture. As we shall see in Chapter Four, corporate culture is either a powerful propellant or an awesome

We are a value-driven organisation, so you wouldn't be able to convince a Volvo engineer to make an unsafe car; he simply wouldn't do it. That consistency of values and consistency of heritage is good because it builds self-confidence, and that self-confidence, at its best, is an open self-confidence that lets other people in, and accepts input from the outside based on the self-confidence that you know who you are.

Leif Johannson,
President & CEO,
Volvo AB

viewed explained that he had done away with the use of internal management letters that for years, had been completed periodically by each country manager. The reports provided a detailed outline of where each location was, relative to plan, key performance indicators, and other pertinent information. It got to the point, however, that both generating and reviewing the reports took so much time that the process had to be re-evaluated. Senior management would have barely gotten through all the reports when the next month's numbers were due: It became a ludicrous exercise.

What soon became evident was that conference calls and one-on-one talks directly with the country managers would prove far more productive than the printed management letters. Conferencing enabled senior managers to match priorities in real time. The management letter is a clear example of a tool that worked well in the past, but in this environment, just won't cut it.

But eliminating an obsolete tool in this case was just the beginning. The CEO has continued to develop the conferencing tool. He now devotes half of his one-on-one conversations to topics other than the business itself. During this time he talks to the individual manager about where he or she is personally, relative to career growth and goals. He starts out by advising them, "I'll let you hear the top two things I've

We have to make sure all the time that we think through "Can we do it a better way?" And also, now after two years, if people start to get a little laid-back on that format, then perhaps you need to change some elements so that it is not so predictable.

*Michael Treschow,
President & CEO,
Electrolux*

Leadership is giving clear strategic direction. You've got to have the right people: You've got to empower your people who are close to customers to drive the organisation.

Mike Grabiner, CEO, Energis

got on my mind and then you can tell me what your agenda is." That way, he makes sure his top managers understand his objectives, and then he discovers things of which he was previously unaware.

This executive has created a new management tool adapted to a quicker environment that has helped his management team become a lot more proactive. It has increased and improved communication within the organisation while reducing the amount of time the communication takes.

A key to survival in today's environment is keeping our antennae up within our own organisations, so that we can "pick up" what needs to stay and what needs to go. It requires the courage to question "truths" that may be held sacred—even though no one can remember why. With external situations changing so quickly, the critical importance of operating within the organisation with a healthy perspective and timely communication can't be overemphasized. Both are essential to successful adaptation to the new environment.

3 Distributed Leadership

IT'S ELEVEN O'CLOCK: WAKE UP!

When Paul was riding to Damascus to imprison another batch of Christians, the Lord, as the story goes, ambushed him. He zapped him from his horse and pinned him down with a blinding light. Paul's headstrong loyalty to the Roman Empire had become a health and safety issue for the young Christian community. "Why do you persecute Me?" boomed the voice within the intense light. Paul did not resist the message; it was pretty much an epiphany for him. He adopted a new set of values that day and aligned himself with a different leader. He put down the weapons of force and picked up sympathy, compassion, and patient persuasion, becoming a leader within the Christian cause.

In a way, the business leadership in Europe is in the process of being knocked from its horse. At the risk of overdrawing the metaphor

> I came here after the former CEO had been here for twenty-five years. He was a strong decision maker, and that was appropriate for the business' needs then. But there were good people here who had never taken any big decisions. It took me one year to really get people believing they could really be the boss in their own divisions and be accountable for their own decisions.
>
> *Flemming Lindeløv,*
> *President & CEO,*
> *Carlsberg A/S*

I am not sure that I see leadership as the role of an individual, but the role of a group of people.

Stephen Raby,
Managing Director,
Stephen Raby Associates

of Paul's holy saga, the message is booming through: Business leadership must change to keep pace with a changing Europe. Chief executives, chairmen, and other leaders of business, must go through a kind of personal epiphany; must recognise that the business environment of the New Europe is so radically mutable, it is no longer good for business to lead us down the same old roads in the same old directions. In fact, what it means to lead—indeed, the very nature of leadership itself—is up for reinvention.

Some, though not many, have already heard the wake-up call and are beginning to reinvent leadership to meet the Web-speed demands of the New Europe. Gary Donahee, EVP and President Nortel Service Provider Solutions, Europe, replaced a chief executive who had demanded staff raise their hands to ask a question in staff meetings. Needless to say, it was a place of very little controversy. Rarely did the senior team openly argue-out decisions. Information was presented and then, behind the scenes, a few people made the decisions.

The company was nowhere on the European map in terms of market presence, nor was it even in the mind-share of potential customers. Yet Europe was then, and remains, one of the hottest growing telecommunications marketplaces on the globe.

ONE IS NOT ENOUGH

So, in comes the new CEO, Donahee, a Canadian who knew very little about Europe, having spent his last assignment in Nortel CALA, their Caribbean and Latin American organisation. Right out of the gate, he was competing with the big boys—Cisco, Lucent, Alcatel, and Siemens; people who know Europe very, very well and had hot, sexy new products. His first realisation was his most important one: The job was too big for him alone, or for any one person. He couldn't make all the decisions about how much to invest in one country or another, whether to joint venture in France or joint venture in Spain, or both. Even to attempt these tasks would mean he'd be travelling and meeting people twenty four hours a day. Meanwhile, the marketplace would slip further from his grasp. Instead, he looked at the slew of good people Nortel had hired and decided to let them lead.

What Gary provided was the motivation to do the job, the clout when his people needed it, and the support of the corporation. He set "big, hairy" stretch targets, helped his people believe they could reach them, and functioned as an ally to help them figure things out. But through it all, he gave them their heads. Gary provided the basics, but the team became the leaders. They were not just managers, not just members of the Nortel Europe Cabinet, but real business leaders. **This is Distributed Leadership.**

We've had a sustained 20 percent year-over-year productivity gain in our business in Europe over the past three years with very very little investment; but by mostly getting people to be properly trained, engaged, and empowered to go do things. And that's an enormous advantage for us. So I think we've got to realise that our financial success is really based on selecting the right people, training them, and really engaging them so it's their business.

Rob Amen, President, International Paper Europe S.A.

A leader has a choice in styles. Different situations require different styles, but you are asking about my general management style. There are times when I have to make the call and be autocratic; but the norm that I am working to is team-based and participative. As the world is becoming more complex, and decisions required faster, I realise that I'm not smart enough to make all the decisions. The leadership challenge is how to get the organisation to flow to get decisions made in an effective and efficient way.

Bill McLaughlin,
Former President & CEO,
Frito-Lay Europe

THIS IS CONFUSION

The turbulent times at Reed Elsevier, by way of contrast, provide a good example of what Distributed Leadership is not! Essentially, when Reed, the primarily UK-based publishing group, and the Dutch publishing company Elsevier merged, they decided to create a power-sharing structure between the two companies led by co-CEOs Nigel Stapelton in London and Herman Bruggink in Amsterdam. While co-heads of companies have worked well in many industries, such as retail, for example, where the chairman is usually the chief merchant and the CEO is usually the operations person, what makes it work is a common culture, clear values, mutual trust, and respect. That was not the case with Reed Elsevier. To make things even worse, the members of the two boards were not aligned either, and in fact, it was in-fighting at the board level that put additional, and unworkable, pressures on Nigel and Herman.

The two corporate cultures were very different and there was neither trust nor respect at the top of either organisation. They lacked a common set of values or a vision to bind them together. Financial and political agendas held sway. And, needless to say, Reed Elsevier's poor performance in relation to its peers was indicative of serious management misalignment at the top. This is not Distributed Leadership; this is petty politics and inflated egos at work, mostly at the board level, leaving both Nigel and Herman between a rock and hard place.

RAPPORT IS THE KEY

Distributed Leadership is not simply a matter of moving the level of control down a notch. It is not "senior teams and junior bosses", a model that emerged from old principles of authority and hierarchy. It is a fundamental shift in thinking toward rapport and the use of Relationship Power, instead of Position Power.

Gary Donahee came into Nortel Europe and replaced the longstanding, rigid formality of Position Power with open dialogue and uncomplicated Relationship Power. He did this because the real business need was for speed; speed of decision making. Rapport is the essential ingredient in all effective relationships. It is through rapport that we feel a connection to each other. It fosters ongoing trust; the feeling that I can say anything to you and you can say anything to me because we know we have goodwill toward each other. In the rapport mode, we share the same values, short-term objectives, and ultimate goals. We trust that together we can find the solutions that best fit the situation; whereas, old-style bossing handed down answers—not necessarily solutions—and made them fit.

The current European business environment is starving for Relationship Power, not the auto-

> It's not about just the chief executive exhibiting leadership. It's creating a culture where exhibiting leadership is accepted as a requirement at all management levels.
>
> *Brian Stewart,*
> *Chief Executive,*
> *Scottish & Newcastle plc*

> I am very keen that people should sit down and talk to us; "How are things going?", "How are you meeting up with your targets?" People know if they are meeting their targets or if they are not. If they are not, then tell them that they are not meeting their targets and help them improve so that they can meet their targets and not come back six months later and still be failing. "What are we going to do about it?"
>
> *Simon Merriman,*
> *Former Director,*
> *Connolly Luxury Goods*

cratic power of the old environment. The new generation of employees are demanding it. The new business environment is one of constant and rapid external change. And the internal changes needed to adapt quickly can come about only with the ability to understand and build relationships. Big change takes a whole lot of trust, respect, and ability to work together in a synergistic kind of way.

The rate of change is so great that companies have had to find ways of creating more intelligence, more knowledge, and of sharing internally. We've moved to a situation now where there are many more points of intelligence, and in a sense, what was once the primacy of leadership is now a much more diffuse responsibility.

David Varney,
CEO,
BG plc

Extraordinary results are the product of extraordinary relationships. If we must accomplish something out of the ordinary, it can be done quickly and easily with extraordinary relationships among the people involved. In the past, knowledge and know-how were much more important than relationships. They were the currency of the last twenty-five years. Now we have to add another denomination: We must develop the ability to form relationships in such a way that people get a whole lot more done a whole lot quicker. Trusting, supportive, and energising relationships are the new currency.

GET OUT OF THE WAY AND
LET RELATIONSHIPS WORK

Everybody knows that there is a great untapped reservoir of power and productivity in the employee body, and everybody is frustrated about how to get at it. There are programmes, empowerment seminars, diversity training—the list is as long as your arm. Most come up short. But when we do get it right, it's like splitting the atom: The company explodes with enthusiasm and effectiveness. David Novak at Tricon Global got it right. Gordon Bethune at Continental Airlines got it right. Gary Donahee at Nortel got it right.

Getting it right happens when leaders first change themselves and come to understand leadership as distributed, rather than centric, power. The CEO must realise that his role as it was once defined—top man, commander, charismatic strong-jawed loner, or the buck-stops-here tough guy—is no longer the most appropriate style for the job at hand. In fact, it's rapidly becoming obsolete. Todays truths are very different from what we were brought up to believe; very different from the way most of us were trained.

An excellent example of a leader changing his thinking and then helping the company change, can be found in Jan Froeshaug, CEO of Egmont, a major magazine publisher and distributor of movies, games and software. By realising that he could not control everything from his headquarters in Copenhagen, Jan understood that the only way to make his growing global organisation effective, and retain top talent, was to practice Distributed Leadership. He set up a series of what he calls

It's got to come from the CEO. He has to very early make it known that the way things work around here is as a team effort. We put egos aside. Everyone has got one, and you don't want to kill their ego, but ego comes second and goal comes first.

Paul Preston,
Chairman,
McDonald's UK

In our country, a CEO is the chairman, meaning chairing the meeting but no more than that. So we try to find a consensus; a way of getting everybody agreeing on a specific approach. That takes time, but of course also creates a lot of commitment from everybody.

Dolf van den Brink,
Member of the Board,
ABN Amro Holding N.V.

"skill teams," in which managers from several different countries, come together as a temporary group to focus on solving common problems facing the company. This gives them the opportunity to be both local leaders and global managers at the same time. Once a solution has been found, they go back to their home regions to implement.

According to Froeshaug, this has the dual advantage of keeping bright people in their home regions, yet at the same time, giving them the exposure and learning that comes from belonging to a global organisation without having to uproot their families and personal lives with frequent career moves.

The future role of the CEO and executive team members is to model and foster open, supportive relationships. This is what releases spirit, energy, and talent. This is what effectively distributes the leadership; first among the top people, then throughout the organisation.

The CEO and senior team must foster more connections between people throughout the company, creating allies and networks with colleagues. They must listen, give respect, gain agreement and alignment, and support and coach. This is not to say they are pushovers or are soft on people. Gary Donahee of Nortel is not soft; he is very direct. But he can also be himself. Jan Froeshaug of Egmont is very direct and a forceful personality, yet he genuinely believes in

It is putting the sense of what is important for the company ahead of what's significant for your particular area. Reflecting what the customer wants in the marketplace is ultimately what's good for the company.

Nicholas Scheele,
Chairman,
Ford of Europe Inc.

getting all the brains in the company to engage on the issues. In fact, true rapport occurs when each party individuates. It is through the integrity of such relationships that Distributed Leadership works, that the culture grows, that the business thrives—not because the CEO holds authority and signs the paycheques.

HOW IT WORKS

In the Distributed Leadership model, business isn't separate from human beings. Business *is* human beings. The corporate culture thrives because a big part of each person's job is to nurture and grow the culture. The culture itself becomes the competitive advantage because people are excited about work, and about opportunity.

DECISION MAKING WITHIN DISTRIBUTED LEADERSHIP

When business *is* human beings, more experience is available to the company, more information and more input are available to the company. As a result, we make better decisions faster. The fundamental truth is this: A team makes better decisions than an individual. A team of players has more access to more relevant information than just one person. Creating a collegiality in

In the coming period of great change and innovation, communication with people is extremely important so that they can adapt and the organisation can adapt. Also, the big job of the CEO is as an agent of change. Vision is one thing, but you have to make it *happen*.

Baron Daniel Janssen,
Chairman,
Solvay S.A.

We are going as far as rewarding mistakes, as long as the learnings of those mistakes are spontaneously being shared with the rest of the organisation leading to new and better projects elsewhere. Because if you support people who make mistakes, you promote risk taking.

John Goossens,
President & CEO,
Belgacom

We are very cohesive as a group, and I think that's why we've been able to handle some of the acquisitions as well as we have done. Teamwork among our senior executives is a big part of our success.

Brian Stewart,
Chief Executive,
Scottish & Newcastle plc

which each person's expertise is required and in which information is shared horizontally, not just from the boss down and back up again, results in better-informed, more innovative, and more practical decisions.

Everybody's catching on to this fact. NASA, for example, has initiated a programme called Cockpit Resource Management which has been adopted by the airline industry. CRM trains pilots to speak to one another; to collabourate on decisions. Too many aircraft have crashed because the captain is not accustomed to taking input from junior officers, no matter how valuable it might be.

In the example of Nortel Europe, Gary Donahee placed people with leadership authority and responsibility out in the marketplace. They gathered information, brought it back to the company, shared it, and used the collective wisdom of the group to make decisions. At the same time, those leaders out in the field were empowered to make decisions because they understood and supported the overarching strategy, principles, values, and goals of the organisation. They didn't need to keep checking with corporate for the boss to hand down a decision.

This is Web-based leadership. If the business environment moves at Web speed, then so must leadership. We have to create a web of networks in our companies between people, wherever they reside. The only way to do this is to bring all the connections together on a frequent basis. If you have trust and openness, then whoever has an issue throws it out into the network, and the best talent chews on it and brings back ideas. Then, if everybody sits and listens, and lets the wisdom of the ideas coalesce, it becomes pretty obvious: Either there is a solution there within the group knowledge and it surfaces, or there isn't, and you throw the questions out again for more information. If the group sense is that they just don't see the solution yet, then a couple of people go back out, get more data, and bring it back. In this system, insight is inevitable. It comes like a blinding flash of the obvious.

I was at a client meeting one afternoon. We broke into groups of three to work on three key business problems. Each was a mixed group that came up with all kinds of different ideas. When people reported their ideas, everybody including the CEO was just a member of the audience, listening, adding information, and giving feedback. The results were far richer than what each small group produced. In this instance, nobody had to make a decision because the decision was obvious. No boss said, "Thank you for your input. Now I will decide." It was simply obvious that we had to use a specific process, then use the heuristic approach (learn-as-you-go) to make the next set of decisions.

You need to have an open-minded culture where you are listening to everyone and you are accepting that you have some clever people in the field, not just sitting in the head office.

Flemming Lindeløv,
President & CEO,
Carlsberg A/S

native to be productive: "My job is to be the loyal opposition or devil's advocate in order to increase the debate,"—blah, blah, blah, and so on. We've all heard it a million times. And we all know that eventually the plot gets lost and our people become demoralised.

By contrast, when we can agree to try something and learn as we go, then that is exactly what happens. We learn and move forward at the same time. We dialogue about the basic possibilities rather than argue every conceivable nuance, until the clearest path for the next three years becomes evident. Hammering out all possible unforeseen details is exactly how the plot gets lost. And that has been the downfall of a lot of European businesses. Their risk-tolerance has traditionally been so low, they have tried to identify every angle in their pursuit of the elusive risk-free path. More often a competitor they never heard of, some young company or a spin-off of a larger company, beats them to the marketplace; and the customer's pocketbook.

IMPLEMENTATION

In the complex and changing environment of today's Europe, real leadership emerges not only in how we make decisions, but also in how we implement them. If you have a culture that can't implement decisions or won't or doesn't exhibit

In pan-European companies, you will have tensions between centralisation and decentralisation. The tensions between people who are learning to work and think individually, who demand that type of individual freedom, who can certainly work very effectively given that latitude and yet the need to still lead, manage, and even "control". And I think that's what makes the future role of the chief executive "different" from what it's been in the past.

Neville Isdell,
President,
Coca-Cola Beverages plc

confidence, flexibility, or accountability, then it falls upon leadership to create such a culture.

Anyone can make a decision: What goes before and what comes after requires wisdom, judgment, and perspective, i.e. "Why should we invest in this or that country or process?", "How much and on what timetable?", "Should it be a sneak attack, or front on?" The Distributed Leadership process illuminates these grey areas because leadership rests with those closest to the specific questions, problems, and possible solutions.

WALKING THE TALK

Shared values communicated through leadership bind people and give them something to believe in together. In the model of Distributed Leadership, everyone walks the talk. Each person becomes a role model of the culture and its values. It is no longer just the chief who has to model. It is now distributed amongst many.

In the old business model, the guy who got great results, constantly beat the budget, and made the company buckets of money without walking the company talk, was generally left alone. In the new business model, the health of the overall culture is of vital importance: It is too costly to the life of the business to support a lone crusader. This guy will need to be coached in the ways of Distributed Leadership, because his contribution, as it stands, is one-dimensional. His job will become tougher. Now, not only does he have to produce results, he must do it in a way that inspires people and upholds the values of the corporation.

Distributed Leadership challenges our old ways of doing things. There's no mistaking the new walk. Compensation programmes, for example, change radically. Gary Donahee, EVP and President, Nortel Service Provider Solutions, has a highly complex, three-dimensional matrix composed of lines of business, accounts, and regional geographies. However, there is only one P&L, which is the total group P&L. And it's the role of leadership at the top to get people to be willing at times to give up their gain so the whole may profit. One line of business might have to donate key technical people to an account team, which means they may lose revenue. But the whole is greater than the sum of the parts.

Compensation can help leverage Distributed Leadership if the weighting and focus is right. In a senior team seminar we facilitated for a large European client, a man stood up and said, "Last year, I didn't get a bonus, yet it was the best year we've ever had as a company. And it was the best year partly because I gave a key group of my people to another business unit, which held the biggest value for the corporation. However, we don't have a compensation system that gives me

So we have got to figure out how to help people understand what the broader picture is. That is too simple a statement to make, but I think it is the most important point.... It is actually just going on time-after-time, and explaining to people that the horizons have shifted somewhat, and that we are all in this together. I guess there are a number of ways we can do that; for example, our company has just made the Senior Management bonus a Europe region performance bonus as opposed to individual country performance.

Martin Glenn,
President & CEO,
Walkers Snack Foods

I find it amusing that I will get a consulting colleague or an investment banker who will sit there and say, "You know, our most important assets go home at night, not like you. Your most important assets are those steel paper machines or paper mills." That's nonsense. Our people are key.

Rob Amen,
President,
International Paper Europe S.A.

any benefit for doing that. As a result, I underperformed, the company had a banner year, and I got no bonus."

Because of the spirit that had built up over time, the team rallied and said, "This is crazy. Let's get in the game together." They agreed right on the spot to create a new compensation system in which individuals contributed 50 percent of their variable bonuses to an overall group bonus.

That is the spirit—and the practical aspect—of Distributed Leadership; how it works. If we distribute information and accountability, we must distribute risk and reward as well.

BUILD IT AND THEY WILL COME

It takes a specific skill level and capability to build leaders throughout the organisation: the way to begin is to build a team at the top. First, build a senior teamwork environment of shared core values and a clear strategy, and distribute the leadership among the players. This takes special focus; we want to distribute leadership, not create additional bosses.

But building a team that can lead in the manner of Distributed Leadership is no easy task, however. A myriad of complex dynamics characterises a top-management team. These are high-calibre people involved in making crucial decisions. They have strong egos and ambitious career goals. Team building among such people takes rare talent and sensitivity. And that is where we must begin.

First, the CEO and senior team must communicate the values and strategies of the company to all employees. Then, they have to back-off from explaining, dictating, and prescribing, and instead lead with their own behaviour. If we provide a business environment with a heavy emphasis on tasks or production, there will be little room for leadership qualities of imagination and innovation; the ability to reflect and think creatively will not emerge. Instead, Distributed Leadership raises the bar and expects everyone, including the CEO, to be innovative, reflective, and introspective. It makes it OK to stop and think; OK to be seen reading a book at your desk. It makes it OK to ask the most important questions, "Why not?" and "What if?"

In Distributed Leadership, the CEO, senior teams, managers, and employees coach, teach, nurture, and support. All are aligned with the strategies, values, and objectives. No one is a clone, but all are alike in fundamental ways. Once everyone, from the chairman to the janitor, knows where the company is going and why, we can rely on our people to practice leadership.

Second, leadership must adopt values that are real living things that matter, not merely posters on the wall or slogans. Leadership then becomes organic; it develops from within. Let me say it another way: If we make everyone in the company

Leading change, as opposed to managing change, means that when, a change needs to be done in the business, and the team at the top is leading that change, they have to start behaving differently. They have to change themselves before they can change the others.

Christiane Wuillamie,
Chairman,
CWB Systems Services plc

You need to motivate people; to share the vision from the management team down to the shop floor. You also need to convince people that is where we want to go, and convince them of the need to change; why we need to change. And you only achieve that by spending a lot of time communicating and listening.

John Goossens,
President & CEO,
Belgacom

aware of where we are going and why we are doing it this way; if each person knows the company's vision, strategy, and goals; its core-competencies and markets—if we communicate all this information to people at all levels, then we don't have to micromanage. Today's leadership is not about management teams, or about the top-down power relationships. Today's leadership is about everybody in the organisation leading.

SO WHAT'S HOLDING UP PROGRESS?

"THE BUCK STOPS HERE"

Two long-held beliefs about leadership create major obstacles to distributing leadership. One is the "buck stops here" sense of supreme responsibility. Most leaders are taken with the fact that they are stewards, that they are being entrusted with a large organisation. So, they think they must somehow do it right. They and only they are held accountable. "I will make certain that things go right," they vow. The fact is, the game is too complex and fast-moving for this belief to be effective.

HEROES AND OTHER MYTHS

The other obstacle is the habit of hero worship. The old leadership model is revered and hon-

My belief is that every single person amongst our 45,000 people inside this company has got a responsibility for providing some form of leadership. When you visit a company, the first person you see is the receptionist and the last person you see is the receptionist. That is a definite leadership opportunity.

Sir Richard Evans,
Chairman,
BAE Systems

oured in mythic John Wayne proportions. We admire the autocrat who has built a successful dynasty-style business. We regard him as a decisive visionary who somehow knows all the right moves, and has all the right answers along with the courage to implement them in the face of great odds. He is larger than life—and we don't give up such a model easily. We need heroes.

The fact is, it's extremely rare for one person to exhibit all those traits. Still, the hope persists to be or find a Bill Gates or Jack Welch or Percy Barnavek or some other exemplary leader. But it's time to let go of that model. First of all, you are going to wait a long time to find that kind of leader. Second, it puts incredible pressure on a leader to expect him to be an Olympian. And finally, though heroes and larger-than-life characters do exist and will always emerge, the pressing web-speed issues facing European business today require the work of many different arms and legs, backs, hearts, muscles, and brains to carry the torch.

MAKING THE MOVE TOWARD DISTRIBUTED LEADERSHIP

Every human being I've ever known prefers working in an environment where they can contribute their ideas as well as their skills; where they are a respected member of the team; where

> We were very much structured on the basis of classic leadership, and we are starting to structure ourselves a bit differently to take in views from outside the company and see how we measure up and benchmark ourselves against others. If you ask me what is the lifeblood of the corporation, I would still say it is leadership. But if you ask me what disease will kill the corporation, I would say it's the absence of benchmarking.
>
> *Peter Job,*
> *CEO,*
> *Reuters plc*

they are trusted to do the right things to move the company forward. So, we are starting with the right raw material: human beings. It so happens that people are hard-wired to perform their best when we are members of a team. The programme is already in place. We just have to recognise the truth: Humans are social, gregarious, learning animals. We are not loners, nor are any of us born chief executives, aspiring to be lonely at the top.

THE TRAINING ESSENTIALS

It is one of the absurdities of corporate life that the higher up we go in the organisation—the greater the level of responsibility and the greater the magnitude of decisions we make—the less training we get. Is this ridiculous, or what? Every airline requires continuing training for pilots. School systems and healthcare organisations require ongoing professional training for their people. Yet most corporate executives who make "Game Over!" decisions on a daily basis get little or no ongoing training after they reach a certain level in the organisation.

Conversely, in the Distributed model, the higher up we go in the organisation, the more training we need, the more information, self-awareness, and personal development we need. The new business environment is going to require more training for senior executives—more than they have ever had, because they are responsible now for greater and greater levels of risk. The old adage applies: "We don't have to be sick to get better."

To initiate Distributed Leadership training, implement management workshops where people can have a shared experience working in a new distributed way. Make it part team building as well. They have to learn about each other because a big part of Distributed Leadership is understanding each other's strengths, weaknesses, and different styles.

It takes a great deal more care and sensitivity to train executive-level teams than is required for product or action teams. The training must help them not only solve today's business problems, but also ground them in a process for achieving outstanding solutions to business problems encountered tomorrow, and the day after that. Once we distribute the leadership, there exists a dynamic process for problem solving: We no longer resort to yesterday's formulas to solve tomorrow's problems.

Training must also provide an opportunity for personal development. It's not all about learning business skills. Executives must have the luxury of sitting back and reflecting on their lives, their business approaches, their habits, their communication and leadership styles. In the past, feedback at the top has been scarce.

> In any big orchestra, you have to have the best soloists feel that they have the right to develop as individuals. And unless you, as the conductor, give them that right and that opportunity, you will not have the best soloists and you also will not have the best orchestra. So there has to be a great amount of freedom and individuality, and you as a conductor have to recognise that there are extremely good professionals in that orchestra. Likewise, if the musicians don't want to play, you can be up there standing, waving your baton forever, and not a single sound will come out of that orchestra.
>
> *Leif Johansson,*
> *President & CEO,*
> *Volvo AB*

Many executives have bought into resisting development by replaying the tape that says, "I must be doing OK because I got here." What else could they think without a system of feedback? Professional development at the top must include personal development.

Distributed Leadership is not a nice thing to do, it's a necessary thing to do. To put it in the coin of the realm, it not only feels better to work this way; it's essential for business.

So, we must have a business reason for Distributed Leadership, and we actually have to initiate the move forward, not just talk about it. We have to create an environment where people can begin training to work in this new way, and we have to build-in the need for coaching from each other. Much courage is needed to stay the course.

COACHING AND FEEDBACK, OR 1+1 = 3

Let's say we agree to run our business according to the Distributed Leadership model. Every person on the team comes in on a different level. Each brings experiences, skills, capabilities, functions, and more or less expertise than the others. Each also comes in with an incredible set of blind spots.

Through a process of coaching and feedback, we begin to see our blind spots. We also begin to recognise and appreciate when we are really

> I am not an instant advocate of co-CEO structures because I think the arrangement can just as easily be achieved by a chief executive who assembles a strong team around him. To create a team which a single CEO leads, but which includes some strong voices that the CEO takes notice of, is the optimal structure. It is probably more optimal than trying to do it with two CEOs, because any business needs a strong message from one person at the top. Perhaps the most difficult part of our co-CEO relationship —particularly with one based in Amsterdam and one based in London—is that even if we think alike, it is not possible, every hour of the working day, to talk alike.
>
> *Nigel Stapleton,*
> *Former Joint Chairman & CEO,*
> *Reed Elsevier*

doing things that contribute to the team and the organisation. This process improves group skills.

Any group gets better first, by playing together, and second, by giving and receiving feedback. One football team plays a schedule of twenty games. After each game, the players all go their separate ways and meet up again the following week to play another game. There is no dialogue, no feedback, no coaching following the games. These players will not develop their strengths, and their team will not become a powerhouse. In contrast, the team that debriefs, talks, asks for help, and gives ideas will grow as a group. This is where 1+1 = 3. Such non-linear interaction breeds wisdom.

It is only through this process of close communication and shared decision-making that a multi-legged, multi-armed leadership of like-minded teams can move the organisation in one clear direction. Organic distributed wisdom sees peripherally, above, and behind, while moving the organisation forward.

We have been working since the beginning of the 90's as a relatively integrated team. It is somewhat inconvenient—for example, the executive VP in charge of specialty chemicals spends a lot of time looking at projects regarding exploration and production that is not directly his concern. On the other hand, a team holds a lot of advantages. First, it creates a strong solidarity concerning the selection of investments. Secondly, integration can provide objective views from people on areas outside their specialisation. This is helpful in that sometimes those in charge of an area can lack distance. Speaking globally, it is very positive to work in this integrated way.

Thierry Desmarest,
Chairman & CEO,
Total Fina S.A.

4 Culture Impacts Performance

Twenty years ago, when I first started to talk about the importance of corporate culture and its actual impact on performance, the usual reply was that culture is the "soft" side of business, and what really counts is the "hard" side: numbers, technology, profits, costs. Up until a few years ago, putting effort into shaping and managing culture was considered merely a "nice thing to do". Only if we have the time and the business is in good shape, so the conversation went, should we think about doing some of that "culture stuff". Today, however, in the fast-moving, highly competitive European business world, a day doesn't go by without an article in the *Financial Times* or *Wall Street Journal Europe* about culture clash, poor performance due to an old culture, or a company's elimination from the marketplace because it responded too slowly to customer needs. Corporate culture, "the way things are done around here", has a huge impact on performance and the ultimate success of the business.

An effective corporate culture is increasingly a source of competitive advantage, which is why we pay such enormous attention to our corporate values; teamwork, respect, integrity, and professionalism.

Dolf van den Brink,
Member of the Board,
ABN Amro Holding N.V.

We were going to enter the Chinese market, and there are a number of ways you can go into China, and the easiest way is actually not to follow the Chinese law. A debate began to happen as to how we should enter the Chinese market, and I was sitting in, listening. And somebody very low in the organisation stood up and said, "We don't do things that way." That shows when a culture works.

Bob Lawson,
CEO,
Electrocomponents plc

OH, NO! DÉJÀ VU...
DÉJÀ VU... DÉJÀ VU...

The following true story comes with a health warning: It may remind you of your own company and cause acute embarrassment!

CULTURE AND THE CUSTOMER

The need: An important customer of an engineering company discovered a technical problem with one of its processes. The objective was to solve the customer's problem and maintain good customer relationships.

The required action: to issue a report to the customer on the nature of the technical issue related to the problem, and provide a solution.

(What follows are the actual minutes of the weekly management meetings concerning the technical solution.)

What Actually Happened:

Week 1:   The management team agrees that a technical report is needed, and Manager X agrees to assign Engineer Y to the task.

Week 2:   Engineer Y misses the agreed deadline.

Look at the changes
that we are going
through right now, and
realise that increasing
change is going to be a
way of life for business.
If you can't have the
senior team aligned, then
you get the stovepipe
effect with some of the
stovepipes being taller
than others. There is then
a lack of common move-
ment forward. This keeps
individuals and everyone
from reaching their
objectives.

Dale Gallagher,
VP Operations,
Frito-Lay Europe

LEARN AS WE GO

A team of players needn't have all the information in order to get going in the right direction.
They make small decisions to get started, and
then, as they implement these decisions, they
discover what works and what doesn't. They
make the next leadership decision based upon
what they have learned.

The point is, if we wait for everything to be
clear, we will never make a decision. What is certain is that in 21st century Europe, everything
will never be clear. But if we set a direction that
people can see is intuitively correct, and if we
share what is happening by coming back into
this network, this web of leadership, and if we
pause a moment to assess what is happening, it
becomes obvious: We just learned some new
information that we didn't have when we started
this. We need to turn right, left, backup, whatever. The next decision becomes clear, and the
next and the next.

DIALOGUE, NOT DEBATE

In a learn-as-we-go Distributed Leadership environment, we align on basic values and goals and
then practice dialogue, as opposed to debate, to
develop ideas, goals, and strategies. The old
debate societies are now too slow and unimagi-

Week 3:	Still no report. Manager X is assigned to chase-up the engineer.
Week 4:	Manager X reports that Engineer Y had not understood the urgency of the report and has now begun; but unfortunately the report is not yet ready for review. He had also been working on some other, more urgent tasks.
Week 5:	The report is complete and has been submitted to Manager X for review.
Week 6:	Manager X was out of the country for the past week and has not had the opportunity to review the report.
Week 7:	Manager X has reviewed the report and identified a fundamental omission. Some further testing is required.
Week 8:	The parts required to carry out the testing are now on order.
Week 9:	The parts will be in this week.
Week 10:	The parts will be in this week.
Week 11:	The parts have arrived, but none

There is only one thing that counts: the right people and the right culture. If you don't have that, you can never compete successfully.

Tom Hedelius, Chairman, Svenska Handelsbanken

Real leadership is the way we do things: it's the values, but then it's actually practising what you preach. It's saying to the organisation, "This is what I want us to do; what we should do", and then demonstrating leadership and creating the culture by acting it out.

John Steele, Group Personnel Director, BT plc

of the offshore engineers is available to carry out the testing.

Week 12:   The testing is complete and the report is being updated.

Week 13:   The amended report is with Manager X for review.

Week 14:   The report is finally issued to the customer. Unfortunately, the completions engineer for whom it was intended has since been transferred overseas. In the meantime, his replacement has found another firm to fix the problem and is thinking of changing suppliers to this new firm.(!)

> The danger of culture is that it becomes a museum piece, and culture, particularly with the speed of change today, has to keep evolving and keep changing. So one of the tasks of leadership is to build flexibility and adaptability into the culture.
>
> *Neville Isdell,*
> *President,*
> *Coca-Cola Beverages plc*

THE BASIC TRUTH—"IT'S THE WAY WE DO THINGS AROUND HERE"

Simply put, an organisation's collective practices—more precisely, those behaviours used to achieve success—comprise its culture. Yes, it's the way we do things around here. But more to the point, it's what employees do when no one is telling them what to do: it's how they respond to customers, to problems, to each other. It's the habitual behaviours that occur. It's the organisational personality whose traits are strong enough to make or break a strategic plan.

We used to think that culture was a soft issue, but the more we see how it impacts performance, that it has everything to do with a competitive edge, the more we see companies struggling with culture as a hard issue. For example, a company like Marks & Spencer, for a long time the premier retailer in the UK, is having a very hard time adapting to modern competitive retailing in Europe, and especially to a customer service focus.

The Marks & Spencer culture has been defined from its beginnings by a very traditional way of doing things. Their loyal customer base has been presumed, as part of the status quo. The culture never had to incorporate a notion such as "earning market share" into its collective understanding. Historically, Marks & Spencer's status had little to do with competitive savvy or speed to market. But, as we well know, things have changed. No business in Europe will be able to presume anything, let alone a loyal customer base built on status. A cultural ideal in a prior era has become a liability today.

IT'S THE CULTURE, !@&!!

Culture is to performance as oil is to an automobile engine: without it, no one goes anywhere. Oil is the life-fluid of the engine, and if it is old and

I think one of our other challenges is to move our top-end management from national to European. We've got to radically change the culture of this business from being a UK-based business that happens to export, to a European business; and it's management team is Electrocomponents first and nationality second. And I don't think we've been able to do that yet.

*Bob Lawson,
Chief Executive,
Electrocomponents plc*

loses its viscosity, having circulated for too long or of low quality, the engine runs rough. It groans and complains at high speeds or on long hauls. It not only performs poorly, it wears out twice as fast as a well-oiled engine. With high-grade clean oil, the engine runs smoothly, even during high-performance demands.

Such is the case with a business and its culture. And no company pays more attention to culture than the new and improved Jaguar organisation. Here's a company that has driven itself from under-performer to miraculous success story. It took most of the last decade, under the leadership of CEO Nick Scheele, to do it; but Jaguar has shot from 34th in quality ranking to an astounding 4th.

Understandably, the Jaguar people want to keep driving success into the new century. So, preparing for the release of the new luxury X400 coming in 2002, in the mid-1990s they began making plans for a suitable manufacturing site. Basically, they had two options: build a new plant, or purchase an existing plant and use its labour force. The second option presented itself in the form of the Ford Escort plant at Halewood, located in an industrialised area of Northwest England known as Merseyside. The major drawback with this option was that the Halewood plant had a history of labour and quality problems stemming back to its very beginning. In fact, the Halewood plant had been on a steady decline as Escort plants

There is no such thing as a perfect organisational structure, there is no such thing as a perfect CEO, and there is definitely no such thing as a perfect culture. You can't take the writings of what has been done in this company or that company in a previous business life and apply it exactly the same. You must build your own high-performance culture that is right for your company and the business. And that is the job of leadership.

John Goossens, President & CEO, Belgacom

in Spain and other parts of Europe were turning out better quality cars with fewer labour problems. On the plus side, this option gave Jaguar and its parent company, Ford, an opportunity to support the Merseyside area and help address its severe unemployment and economic issues.

One of the most economically challenged areas in Britain, Merseyside is the ideal site for building the new Jaguar model. The new Jaguar production facility will create and secure much-needed jobs and boost the local economy, all while bringing Merseyside a dose of prestige. The British government has even been willing to contribute substantial funds to support the region. But many Jaguar executives were suspicious of the plan because of Halewood's history. The Halewood culture stems from the socialist dock strikes of the 1950s and has in many ways ruled the region ever since. The plant culture at Halewood was further entrenched in resistance and negativitiy as a result of the rather draconian management tactics employed by Ford. It's no surprise that Ford, using a traditional top-down, rule-driven management style, never really created a winning culture there. The plant consistently performed poorly while Ford management ran itself ragged, putting out the many fires of labour strikes and threats of closings.

The big hurdle, then, was whether or not the Halewood culture could be reshaped into a

We are centralising in many areas to have greater efficiency. But the fact is, consumers actually are becoming more local, more regional; so we actually have to rationalise and localise what we are doing as well.

Neville Isdell,
President,
Coca-Cola Beverages plc

> The Jaguar culture is tremendously important. Frankly, without it we wouldn't have survived. The Jaguar culture is first, a recognition of heritage and history. There is a tremendous recognition of heritage, a putting of the customer first. If you go around the world, there is very much a Jaguar family feel within the company. It's present among dealers, customers, suppliers, and all the people within Jaguar—we share mutual objectives and heritage, as well as a mutual history and future.
>
> *Nicholas Scheele,*
> *Chairman,*
> *Ford of Europe Inc.*

Jaguar Quality culture. Undaunted by the culture challenge and smelling opportunity, Jaguar asked the most important question: "What if?".... "What if we go to Merseyside and commit to building the X400? What if we try to turn a suspicious, protective, and defensive culture into one of open communication, trust, teamwork, pride, and diversity? The motor industry in Britain is not diverse in any way—so far. But what if we create a culture that includes, rather than excludes, talent—male and female, Asian, black, and white—and thereby make ourselves the beneficiary of the best talent available? What if we could take the already existing experience base at Halewood and create a positive, high-performance culture where we can get the best out of everyone, and give them back a great place to work as well as improved education and training? What if?"

Enthused by the vast possibilities raised by such a strong "What if?", the British government is supplying monies to support Jaguar's entrance into Merseyside. The union, too, has sat down with the new management in an effort to find some common ground from which to get the enterprise rolling.

Now, we can't tell the end of the Halewood story—yet. Most likely, we won't know until well into 2004. It is a work in progress, but a recent article in the December 1999 edition of *AUTOCAR* magazine hints at the transformation that is taking place inside Halewood. Recently Halewood was acknowledged by Hughes Research Worldwide for its dramatic culture change over a one year period.

The story of the initial successes at Halewood is really the story of Jaguar's enlightened commitment to addressing the issue of culture and cultural transformation. Culture and performance go hand in hand, for better and for worse. Without attention to a healthy culture, business organisations will not make it up the steep hills of the new century.

CULTURE: THE DNA OF THE ORGANISM

Culture is the DNA of every organisation. Each time the company grows, it's the culture that replicates itself. It is incredibly strong. It characterises the collective beliefs about the best ways to solve business problems. When outsiders come into a culture, they are quickly assimilated and acculturated. At first, the new person spends time observing "how things are done around here", and how this place is different from their former environment. Then, fairly soon, an all-but-unconscious mechanism kicks in. They want to be a part of the group. Certainly what they *don't* want is to be the odd guy out. Before long, they become a part of the culture.

In our organisation, clear communication, both top-down and bottom-up, is a critical part of maintaining a strong, clear corporate culture. Another key component of our culture is our insistence on respect for everyone in the organisation, no matter the level or department in which they work. Everyone and every job is important, whether in sales and marketing or cleaning our facilities.

Hugo Vandamme,
President & CEO,
Barco N.V.

POLICY SCHMOLICY! WHAT ARE THEY SAYING AROUND THE WATER COOLER?

The corporate culture gets transmitted by what I call the unwritten ground rules. Companies function on two sets of standards: the written and the unwritten rules. The written rules consist of the the text of the annual report, the contents of employee manuals, or the "vision" and "mission" statements proudly displayed in the reception area. The written rules can be read and referenced: "Look, here it says blah, blah and so forth in the employee handbook, and therefore such and such should or shouldn't be happening."

But it is the *unwritten* rules that are more important to the individual employee. Apart from generalised performance ideals or admonitions against inappropriate behaviours, the manual won't tell an employee the real deal. The organisation promotes some people, fires others. The real reasons are rarely outlined in the employee manual. The official manual also doesn't divulge the informal operational scheme for getting things accomplished within the organisation. It is the unwritten rules that tell us that a certain person or department, for example, might have to get involved first or any effort will die on the vine. The unwritten rules tell us where the roadblocks are, and who is going to get the job done; and how.

There also seem to be, in most cases, two separate and distinct codes of conduct that coexist

Whether Europe is treated as a whole or whether it is separate on a legal basis; there are still going to be cultural differences, and no legislation is going to account for that.

Stephen Raby,
Managing Director,
Stephen Raby Associates

in corporate environments: the printed organi-sational chart and the informal network. Official procedures often bring little to bear on how things actually get done and on what truly hap-pens during the course of the workday. So the problem of task fulfilment within a culture can be a major issue. Another difficulty lies in incon-sistencies between prescribed and real behaviour practices. I've seen too many companies that have clear policies on conduct and integrity framed in parchment and detailed in manuals, but two of the VPs are having affairs with their secretaries and everybody knows it.

Manuals and policy statements pale against leaders' behaviour.

Many times, I have coached people who want to find out what is really going on in a company to pay closer attention to gossip than to formal statements. Ask the company's customers. Listen to what peo-ple are whispering at the water cooler. Check out the jokes circulating on email. Informally, people will reveal what they believe and provide the most accurate insight into the culture's true nature.

CULTURE MATTERS

First and foremost, a healthy culture is a competi-tive advantage. The current race-paced, techno-logical environment in Europe has created what McKinsey & Co. calls "the war for talent". There

> The cultures of Globecast Northern Europe and Globecast Paris are com-pletely different. I can't tell you how different they are. We are miles apart culturally. One of our core objectives is to bring those cultures closer together, yet still offer diversity of service. You have to remain able to provide the local culture with what they want, and that means adapting to each of the local areas. On a global basis, you have to provide a balance between the American, the UK, and the French culture.
>
> *Sarah Williams,*
> *CEO,*
> *Globecast Northern Europe Ltd*

It is simple mathematical projection; in the year 2010, in Europe, you are going to have less available talent. But the demand for good talent will continue to grow fast. My guys are constantly under pressure from headhunters, entrepreneurs, you name it. And I am not sure that we have a good system to retain talent. It is probably good, when compared to other companies, but I worry it is not good enough.

Marco Jesi,
President,
Frito-Lay Southern Europe

is fierce competition for the most skilled, highest-quality executive and management talent available.

The fact is, high-quality people change jobs, but not simply for more money. Cultural attributes motivate job changes to a great extent. People want to work for a company that will truly nurture and grow them; where they will fit in, and be a part of a great team and make a difference. People want to be part of a healthy, high-performance culture that can attract more of the best people. A company becomes known as a fantastic place to work, and word gets out. Culture can be a secret weapon in the war for talent.

Culture determines how much productivity and outside-the-box thinking an organisation gets from its people. It either fosters or diminishes such critical success factors. Everything great talent offers—innovation, problem solving, ideas, flexibility—links with the corporate personality.

Culture also really matters when it comes to implementation. Culture can either speed or hinder it. And, as I pointed out in the introduction, speed of implementation is the new currency in today's economic environment. Our business environment is moving at Web speed. A culture that slows things down—through overdone hierarchy, poor teamwork, lack of alignment at the top and therefore through the ranks, confused responsibilities, or internal back-biting and competition—short-circuits efforts and keeps its company out of the race.

THE JAWS OF CULTURE

Among clients and the business community in general, we see lots of great strategies, impressive re-engineering plans, and excellent opportunities to implement new ideas that never get off the ground. Even the most ingenious ideas have difficulty passing through the jaws of culture. Culture is so strong that it chews them up, just as Spielberg's shark did the swimmers on that cinematic Long Island beach.

Hundreds of change-initiative task forces have been started, only to disband in defeat; rejected because the culture won't assimilate new and unfamiliar ideas foisted upon it—no matter how ingenious they are. Sometimes ideas reach the second stage—where they get nitpicked to death because the culture is one of debate rather than of dialogue and improvement. A friend of mine said of such an experience, "In this culture, you don't die quickly, you die by a thousand cuts. We

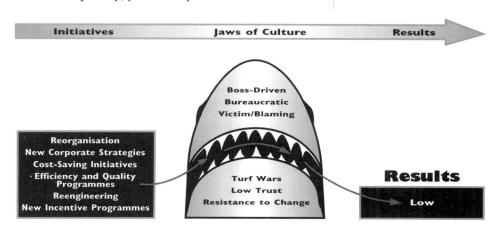

How do you make people who have traditionally been great nationalistic flag carriers, become still highly focused employees, but with a broader European perspective?

Sir Peter Bonfield,
Chief Executive,
BT plc

debate until everybody bleeds to death." It's a culture where nothing ever gets accomplished or implemented.

YESTERDAY'S WAYS SINK TOMORROW'S IDEAS

In the old Europe, relatively little changed. Competition did not sway daily consideration much. No matter what difficulties an organisation faced, it was a safe bet that at some point, not too far down the road, the key elements of strategy, structure, and culture would align.

Not so when the businesss environment begins to change at Web-speed, as it has in new millennium Europe. Today's global marketplace has forced a new focus on strategy, because strategy directly addresses competition. Aligning the three essentials of strategy, structure, and culture makes running a successful business much easier. But in 21st century Europe, achieving that alignment will not be the simple reorganisation exercise it once was.

A good CEO must pay attention to the needs and interests of young employees today in entrepreneurship, and create an organisation which is able to attract and retain these people.

Hugo Vandamme,
President & CEO,
Barco N.V.

Competition is no longer a mere item on the agenda of business. It is a primary, global business force to be constantly reckoned with. In order to survive, a company needs to determine a new, and effective, tactic to win the race for business. Top-level executives must spend a great deal of time revising strategy; whether in the form of increased customer focus, speed to market, brand diversification, or developing a more pan-European, and ultimately global, posture. Complex, tough questions arise: whether to decentralise, to form a matrix structure, or to replace country managers with account managers. The strategy has to be developed quickly and it must be right for the new face of European business. Then it must pass through the real culture before it gets fully implemented.

Calamity strikes, and strikes hard when we try to implement a new strategy within an old culture. It is like a trying to win a race in a speedboat that's towing a freighter.

We can't implement tomorrow's ideas with yesterday's thinking. A company cannot expect its people to behave in a different way unless its people begin to think in a different way, believe different things, and hold different values. Leadership has to infuse new thinking into the culture in order to get new conduct. Otherwise, in the face of change an organisation's own culture becomes a monstrous, sea-roaming carnivore.

THE CULTURAL PANOPLY OF
EUROPE: THE COMPETITIVE EDGE

The reality facing us, if anyone wonders, is that Europe is not the United States of Europe and probably never will be. It is a big marketplace but

The traditional German business culture is very collegiate in nature unlike that of U.S. companies where the chairman and CEO tend to run the show. In this type of environment, communication within the organisation is a core part of its corporate culture. Effective communication is something to which we give a lot of thought at Dresdner Bank and permeates the organisation from the board level downwards. While members of the board at Dresdner Bank have portfolios for which they are responsible, we all come together to make key decisions.

Gerd Häusler,
Chairman,
Dresdner Kleinwort Benson

Carlsberg is both a global company and a local company—we call ourselves "Glocal"! And it is important to have an overall culture and values, but be able to adapt your product and your marketing for the local marketplace.

Flemming Lindeløv,
President & CEO,
Carlsberg A/S

not a unified one, and certainly not characterised by the similarities shared by the States. A company that believes it can instantaneously create a homogeneous, pan-European culture is in for a rude shock. It just doesn't happen that way. No one can mandate a common culture or a common set of processes. And who would want to? We need diversity. Local flavour and cultural approaches are essential if Europe is to beat out its global competitors. There is great richness in the diversity of European social cultures, and therefore in the varieties of opportunity within market and customer preferences. And the critical question of how the customer wants to be served depends on the local culture.

CREATING A BALANCED EUROPEAN CULTURE

Meeting Local Needs with Global Vision

Our dialogues with leaders have led us to the conclusion that the successful pan-European organisation will be characterised by having one overarching Culture (big "C") that binds everyone together. At the same time, it must also have respect for and foster local, market-sensitive cultures (little "c's") that keep the organisation focused on the most important ingredient in the business success formula: local customers and their needs. Both are required for effectiveness in the new competitive European marketplace.

Executives can't assume that loyalty, pride, and team spirit emerge because the corporate logo is emblazoned on paycheques, or that a balance sheet and common name automatically builds a competitive, big-picture culture. Leaders must create the kind of affiliation that produces pride and excitement about belonging to a "bigger game"; something that gives employees an opportunity to make a bigger difference in the world. At the same time, globally savvy leaders encourage and perpetuate small, community cultures because of their market-sensitivity and responsiveness. But—and this is important— they do so while building a larger vision.

I recently received a holiday card from one of the Frito-Lay Europe snack food companies, UZAY GIDA. It was a colourful card, showing with pride the transition that was taking place as they changed their brand name from UZAY GIDA to Frito-Lay. While this was obviously a part of a global branding alignment to draw on the positive impact of a power brand, it also showed a significant cultural shift taking place, and pride at belonging to a much bigger game. Here is the text from the card:

I think that the whole approach to markets will change enormously; where, if "national" becomes less of an issue, then "local" may become even more of an issue, with the European-wide perspective at one end and the very local perspective at the other end.

Helen Alexander,
CEO,
The Economist Group

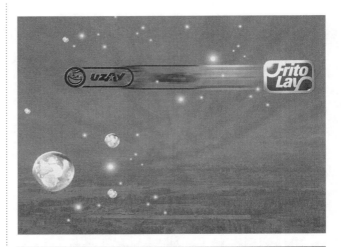

Our company, which has been the pioneer of salty snack production for many years under the name UZAY GIDA Sanayi ve Ticaret A.S., is now becoming universal and will from now on operate under the name Frito-Lay Gida Sanayi ve Ticaret A.S.

Welcome Frito-Lay Türkiye.

This is the task of leadership in the new, pan-European business environment: to create a balanced Big "C"–Little "c" culture, a culture in which people not only retain local pride and connection, but also gain access to a new, superordinate approach to doing business, and are excited and motivated by the opportunities to play in a bigger game.

In a big "C" culture, people have the opportunity to improve the company by delivering ideas, listening to each other, and working together across traditional departmental or even national boundries. Despite their differences, they are united under the banner of their company's bigger vision and a set of values that states how this company affects the world outside of business—the local community, the environment, the schools, the larger world. In this culture, people make a difference within a company that is making a difference in the world.

Global marketing involves global initiatives, marketing initiatives, and product distribution. But besides that, I think the rest become continuously local and regional efforts.

Michael Treschow,
President & CEO,
Electrolux

A SPIN IN THE CULTURAL BLENDER

Every pan-European company needs a strategy to build a larger vision. Some leaders toss groups together and then try to find the common ingredient. This can create a "blender" effect, which usually appeals to the lowest common denominator and tries to please everybody. What it usually yields is an unappealing, bureaucratic puree.

The goal is not that everyone be the same. The goal of leadership must be to ensure that the greater good involves all the different parts of the company in such a way that they create something greater than their sum: an effective pan-European high-performance organisation that truly makes a difference in the business world.

Traditionally, Europe has focused too much on its separate cultures. While this may be a controversial statement, overdone nationalism is the single biggest stumbling block for creating truly pan-European organisations. Leadership's job is to turn that kettle upside-down and focus on a larger vision—the big "C". Then all the national differences can function as they should; to provide context, not obstacles.

LEADERS CHEER ON THE BIG "C"

Giving diverse regional groups access to the larger vision will be crucial in the new European environment. Scope and scale can be fostered only by a pan-European approach. Michael Treschow, Electrolux's CEO, faces a tough situation especially. He's got to get people excited about its products cross-culturally and on a larger scale. How can the company build a culture in which individuals feel they make a difference? I'm willing to bet Electrolux will find an overarching set of global values to unite people in pursuit of a larger vision while also building on the company's success in the local markets.

Employees as well as executives also need to see

> The interesting challenge is to find the balance among my staff, functional leaders, and the field generals. The functional team is driving for synergy, harmonisation and common processes. The line executives are striving to satisfy and connect with local consumers and customers. Ours is a competitive environment so we need the efficiencies that come from scale, and ours is a consumer business that, though becoming more European, has strong local roots.
>
> *Bill McLaughlin,*
> *Former President & CEO,*
> *Frito-Lay Europe*

how they will gain from being part of a globally focused company. Greater opportunities to grow, learn, and develop can excite and motivate people, as well as give them the chance to learn other jobs and advance laterally while increasing skill levels. Within organisations like McDonald's Europe, people are recruited into a growing, pan-European organisation that fosters local cultures and stimulates local economies. It gives jobs to people who otherwise would not have them. These employees can have pride in their work. They are not merely "flipping burgers" or even just earning a pay cheque; they are creating a strong national economy. They are doing good by contributing to a larger vision; a stronger economic base for their own, often low-income social culture.

Promoting the big "C" is the job of leadership, pure and simple. No other group in the organisation can do it. Leaders have to talk it, believe it, and talk it some more. It has to be a part of every speech, a rallying cry: "We belong to something great. Collectively, we do something great."

THE GOOD NEWS: HUMANS
WILL BE HUMAN

A fundamental human condition, that we are all social beings, helps leadership reshape corporate culture. We all have an innate desire to be part of something bigger; a primordial or primeval

At Lego, I made a statement to all the companies we had throughout the world at that time, and said, "We are part of the local environment but we are also part of the global environment; so what we do locally reflects how we are perceived globally."

Vagn Holck Andersen,
Chairman,
Interdan A/S

impulse, if you will, to work together to improve our lot in life. That impulse serves both the small "c's" and the big "C."

The social impetus toward the greater good feeds the creation of a pan-European organisation. In it, opportunities exist that otherwise would not. Today's organisations are becoming broad and flat: there are fewer upward slots for advancement. But, as mentioned previously, greater opportunities for lateral development and progression can be had in pan-European companies. This then becomes a new frontier, offering expansion of skill sets and informational access on an unprecedented scale.

A NEW LEADERSHIP DIMENSION

In the old days, leadership was simpler. It involved a choice between the right way and the wrong way of doing things. The leader only had to identify which was which. Now the task of leadership is more complex. Often, the decisions we face involve a choice between two right approaches. For example, should I reorganise my business to be product-driven or account-driven? Either choice will work, but which will work best within the context of my company and culture? I can bring either of two products to market within ninety days. Both satisfy the customers' needs and fit within our local cultural

> The CEO who is not conversant in European languages will have problems being properly accepted. Anybody who tries to make a bigger European market on the basis of an English language tradition will find it difficult. I do believe that the CEO of the future in Europe has to be a real European, familiar with all the aspects of Europe, including the eastern part of Europe. Eastern Europe is a great growth area, and the CEO of the future has to be familiar, at least to some extent, with languages and ways of thinking in these countries.
>
> *Peter Job,*
> *CEO,*
> *Reuters plc*

needs. Again, either choice, on the surface, is right. The best decision might well depend on whether the culture can make a specific adjustment. The process of leading requires information that must be derived from the culture; it requires knowing and guiding the culture.

Successful leaders understand and assimilate cultural factors in decision making; they know implementation will work only within a cultural context.

One Leader's Approach

The new chairman of Munich-based Giesecke & Devrient, the world's second-largest bank note printer, has not only recognised this challenge, but also made clear his intention to deal with it. Willi Berchtold joined his 147-year-old company after twenty years with IBM's European operations. His training in the U.S. company made him "success-oriented", he says, and his goal with Giesecke & Devrient is to open up a company that traditionally has played it close to the vest. The security demands of the business—cash handling, printing at high-security facilities, and a competitive "smart card" division—have engendered and continue to fuel a secretive culture. The company's tendency to be reclusive has long been justified as necessary. Berchtold wants to change all that. His aim is to create more open, interactive lines of communication

I believe in the power of a team, provided that the team, and that means everybody, has a speciality and together they are worth more than each individual in the team. What I don't believe in is a collegiate decision. I believe very much in the final word sitting with somebody. But this does not imply that this somebody is always right. The real responsibility of a leader is to get the best decisions out of the culture and to gain commitment.

Georges Jacobs,
Chairman, Executive Committee,
UCB S.A.

among staff, making them more responsive to new ideas and business trends. In this way, he believes he will make the company more globally competitive and increase profits. He wants nothing less than to change the face of the company while continuing to be private. How difficult will it be? How will he do it?

First, he is not trying to do it alone. He has put his current management staff on an incentive programme. Since the existing day-to-day nature of the business will change drastically with advances in technology—software, telecommunications, and payment networks—he set a goal of hiring five hundred technology experts by 2000. It is his belief that they not only will provide the technical expertise the company needs to compete in the global, technological marketplace, but also will spark a cultural shift to the openness he sees as essential to a competitive edge.

His immense challenge will be to make the culture see and believe in the necessity of expanding and becoming part of something bigger: a globally competitive organisation; an active participant in the big "C."

It's the Customer & ?#%!!

Let's say leadership has done all its work building a compelling story that inspires the culture to see the bigger vision. At what point do all the various small "c" cultures meet? What is their

> I think the real issue about companies and their competitive structure is whether they can actually rationalise and be truly competitive on a global scale. That doesn't have as much to do with scale, as it has to do with being able to instil a performance culture into the company. Then I think the other issue has to do with the ability to manage people. To me, the real successful companies in the 21st century are going to be those whose people can deal with a multi-cultural organisation.
>
> *Leif Johansson,*
> *President & CEO,*
> *Volvo AB*

common ground? It must be the customer!

No matter our nationalities, no matter our previous cultures, adjusting our focus to the customer reveals that we are all trying to accomplish the same thing. Our single point of contact is the customer.

Focusing on the customer neutralizes those momentum-killers; internal politics and envy— who's got the bigger window, the better view, the bigger chunk of the budget. Other morale problems fade as well, or don't even develop such thorns in the side as tardiness, late-starting meetings, neglected agendas, and people's reluctance to contribute ideas.

Instead, everybody sees that they are part of the same opportunity: to serve and satisfy the customer better than the competition can. Leadership's job is then to motivate everyone to focus on customers.

Organisations increasingly will have to find ways to attract and retain people from different cultures in the world in order that the large global institutions, such as companies in which Investor A/B has stakes, can play locally by the local rules, yet realise the cross-border benefits of being global. We call it a "multi-domestic" organisation.

Jacob Wallenberg,
Chairman,
SE Banken Group

Performance with a Capital "P"

With an overarching big "C" culture of shared common values, and a focus at all levels on the customer, the business performs better. Making decisions is easier. The system contains less noise. Such traditional pitfalls as posturing over the French way versus the German, or the need to assign committees to make sure "A" doesn't step on "B's" toes, tend to fall by the wayside. Implementation is faster than when decisions and methods are based on the politics of national cultures. Feedback from the market-place arrives more quickly; adjustments are made earlier and more smoothly.

When we speak about culture and performance, we don't concentrate only on getting the numbers we want, but also on areas like customer service, new ideas, the spirit that attracts new talent: an environmentally stimulating situation providing growth. Business is about making money, but that is not the only measure of success. Work has to become more than just a place to work. It's a place to socialise, to learn, to hone our skills, and to satisfy our basic human need to make a difference.

Frito-Lay in Europe: An Approach that Worked

When Frito-Lay wanted to build a European presence, it began by acquiring snack food companies in ten or twelve European countries: Walker's Crisps, C&K, Smith's Foods, and Matsutano, with chips and biscuits in Spain and Portugal, and even UZAY GIDA in Turkey. Frito-Lay Europe was born, but the postpartum could have developed into a major depression.

It started as a collection of different brands, cultures, ways of operating, systems, standards, recruiting sources, and factories. In the U.S., of

Global competitiveness is the key to wealth generation and all the good things we want to do in society, so there is no doubt that Europe has got to be global. That's where the future lies, but I think our progress in getting there is remarkably slow.

David Varney,
CEO,
BG plc

course, Frito-Lay could mass-market and get the results it wanted. But in Europe, the company had to attend to dozens of smaller markets stemming from local cultures with varied tastes and preferences. The critical question was how to build a pan-European organisation from this hodgepodge.

The leaders took a series of steps. First, the presidents of the acquired companies, many of whom had never met, came together for a workshop on teamwork and alignment. They had a new CEO, Bill McLaughlin, an American who had never worked in Europe before. He realised instantly that his "team" members all had their own, very different cultures and ways of doing business. His first goal, then, was to encourage these powerful personalities to form a cohesive team to learn about and respect each other.

Next, he tried to develop trust and understanding. He had them work together to develop a tradition, and then a set of values. The group decided how to run the business, and set economic and other operational and organisational goals.

Clearly, Frito-Lay would need to shift from multiple brands to a common one with local presences. They began the slow process of re-badging and printing the Frito-Lay "sun and banner" logo on the packages. Uniform standards and processes for products were set, and manufacturing methods and quality standards were established. The result? The customer got higher-

I don't think that local customers care about where call centres or administrative centres or logistics or factories are are located, as long as they receive the service they need.

Michael Treschow,
President & CEO,
Electrolux

quality products and began to recognise and choose the "sun and banner" as favourite brands.

BUILDING A SUCCESSFUL CULTURE

At this stage, Frito-Lay's new management began collapsing organisations and building centralised marketing efforts, pushing brand and quality hard. Local sales reps helped identify specific cultural preferences; for example, people in Spain liked different flavourings than people in Holland. Some countries liked salty snacks, some sweet. Frito-Lay Europe recognised taste was a local issue and capitalised on it.

The company acknowledged and showed respect for small "c" values. But it built its presence in Europe on the notion that each individual could belong to something bigger. United, they could become the greatest snack food company in Europe.

The resounding reality for individuals was that as participants in the larger vision, they would learn more, acquire expanded skill sets, and become more employable than they were as members of the small "c" organisation.

Early results were strong. Work-life improved. Country managers who prior to the acquisition had dealt with administrative, manufacturing, and quality headaches, could now focus on sales and customers. The headaches were relieved by a cen-

> Unless you've got people really committed to each other's success, you can't possibly respond fast enough. You will get there in the end, but others will get there a lot quicker than you. It's really important to get people locked together and committed to each other. That's a critical role of the CEO —to manage that dynamic.
>
> *Mike Grabiner,*
> *CEO, Energis*

tralised, specially trained support organisation. The tough job of global leadership paid off.

Global One's Not-So-Global Approach (Which Didn't Work)

Global One, a joint venture between France Telecom, Deutsche Telekom, and Sprint, tried to build a Global One culture, but it was constantly undermined by the tumultuous relationships between the shareholders. While there were good people from all the companies trying to work together, and doing some good work for their customers, the shareholders seemed to insist that each of the three companies be fully represented with their own policies and even keep some of their own operating systems. Employees retained tight links to their parent company, so they always had a back door. The common culture and a set of shared values was published, but was never really allowed to be built. People weren't identified as "Global One people". They were France Telecom, or Deutsche Telekom, or Sprint people, working for Global One. If a Global One employee was asked which company he or she worked for, the reply was the former company's name.

All the separate factions concentrated on their differences; on issues that alienated them from each other. Debates over how much better their own, old ways were, frequently reached a fevered pitch. A fiasco from the outset, featuring hor-

I think Europe will change from thinking about not best of breed in the UK, or best of breed in France or Germany, but having to think far more broadly about European benchmarking.

Brian Larcombe,
President & CEO,
3i Group plc

The major difference between today and five years from now is that the early movers will have either become, or be in the process of becoming, much more transnational. You will have an enormous rationalisation going on, because there is such duplication of tasks across the European continent and they will be rationalised.

Jan Froeshaug,
Group President and CEO,
Egmont International Holding
A/S

rendous politics and slowness to market, Global One was one of the most poorly implemented great ideas in the history of business. Operating losses have been estimated at several hundred million dollars. Ironically, what stretched out the agony was the very fact that the companies involved had deep pockets.

The Inevitable Culture Challenge: Mergers and Acquisitions

A phenomenon present in the United States for the past five years has finally reached Europe: the mega-merger. European business people have adopted a popular saying, "Size *does* matter." The way you grow quickly is not through organic development, but through acquisition. In the first six months of 1999 alone, European cross-border mergers and acquisitions surged to $167 billion, up from $100 billion the prior year. Europe is consolidating. Morgan Stanley predicts that the value of M&A activity in Europe could reach $1 trillion by 2000.

Not too surprisingly, the leaders of Europe are wary, all too aware of the dismal record of failed mergers and acquisitions in the U.S. Most M&As have been painful experiences that haven't worked very well. Even so, the merger race has not slowed in the U.S. By mid-year 1999, U.S. M&A volume had exceeded $880 billion, on its way to matching 1998's record $1.6 trillion.

Many European executives emulate and actively seek training in U.S. management tactics, which puts them in the perfect position to learn from America's costly mistakes. Most mergers are like two people who get married based on age, height, and IQ, then realise they can't live together because they are so different. Perhaps the most critical, most overlooked issue in the M&A process has been an understanding of cultural patterns and different corporate cultures. The idea of cross-border mergers only adds to the complexity.

European leaders must pay attention to culture, learn its currents, and determine how it relates to performance. This process begins by developing "culture audits", or corporate culture profiles for the companies involved, to help avoid the culture clash. To do this, it becomes imperative to look at cultural compatibility as well as the financials.

The following example is a culture profile of two actual companies who are planning on merging. What would you say they must pay attention to during the integration process? How different or similar are these two cultures? (See figure Two Merging Telecoms.)

Once cultures are identified and the merger is underway, leaders have before them three of their most critical tasks: communicate, communicate, communicate.

Effectively, Americans are able to manoeuvre and make many mistakes because they have such a massive market, and Europeans confine themselves to small markets and splintered markets and have to pursue a more cautious policy. I don't think we can get by any longer like that.

Peter Job,
CEO,
Reuters plc

Two Merging Telecoms

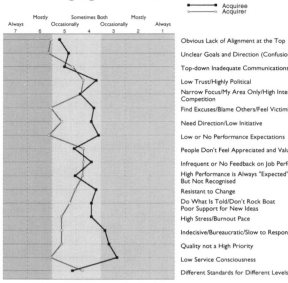

TALK TO ME, I'VE BEEN ACQUIRED

Unclear and shifting reporting structures characterise most failed mergers, according to *Mergers & Acquisitions* magazine. Successful acquisitions, by contrast, feature well-communicated chain-of-command relationships established early on and changed rarely, if at all. Without these open and secure lines of communication, people become closed and insecure.

No one likes awaiting some impending event, especially without knowing for sure what it is or how it is likely to affect his or her well-being or day-to-day existence. An apt story illustrates this:

A spy is captured behind enemy lines. The commandant offers him two choices: the firing line or passage through a mysterious black door at the far end of the courtyard. After hours of perspiration and deliberation, the spy chooses to face the firing squad—a known quantity—at dawn. When he is permanently out of his misery, a Red Cross worker asks the commandant, "What was behind the black door?" "Freedom", the commandant replies.

People prefer the known to the unknown. They can adjust, prepare, and do whatever they need to—as long as they know what they are up against. In order to adapt individual perspectives to the larger vision, European managers will have to nurture and communicate goals and desired adjustments over and over again.

Communication during the merger of two cultures cannot be overrated. Harvard professor and psychologist Harry Levinson has found that mergers, though offering individuals greater opportunities, are nevertheless often perceived as a threat to one's equilibrium. However positive the new outcome, the world as one knows it is ending.

Without an ongoing, earnest communication effort, leaders can expect a stubborn "us against them" mentality to define their new joint-culture. It is critical to identify positive cultural factors—or new, similar traits—in both

I think if you talk about successful companies, the key is going to be understanding what the possible alternatives are for direction in the EU, and being able to have strategies to address alternative realities in the marketplace.

Dale Gallagher,
VP Operations,
Frito-Lay Europe

organisations, and to emphasise and foster them in the new structure.

Culture: The Last Frontier?

By this point, we have seen how culture not only matters, it is essential in determining our performance in local and global business markets. "Getting it right" is a monumental task that takes leadership and a lot of teamwork. But let's say we've done it. Our big "C" culture is established or merged, led by a larger vision that values local culture as well. It is adaptable and healthy, to boot. The organisation is thriving. Can leadership now, finally, take its well-deserved rest?

Not by a long shot.

Chapter 5 will explore the ways that, with the culture intact, that leadership must take the next critical step to ensure that brand and culture match.

5 Brand & Culture Must Match

THE STORY OF THE BAD TRIP

A European senior executive was travelling in the States some time ago and booked a flight with the airline whose brand image promised *The Friendly Skies*. What their advertising assured customers was, "We are friendly. We are on your side. We will do anything to help make your trip pleasant."

After check-in, our executive headed for the business-class lounge where she planned to get online, make some phone calls, and relax with the paper. But the door to the lounge was padlocked and on it was taped a sign that said, "Closed Until Further Notice. We are renovating our lounge to give you greater comfort." There the executive stood, locked out of the place she had hoped to catch her breath. And all she got from the *friendly skies airline* was the explicit message "You can't come in here", and

At TV3 I realised it was magic. If you spent a lot of time working with people, explaining and trying to think out comprehensive models for what we are doing, people that slept at work suddenly woke up and started to do things and a lot of decisions became easy. You can see that you will increase profit and save a lot of money if people in the culture understand what the brand is.

Per Bystedt,
Chairman,
Spray Razorfish

the implicit message "Too bad, go away, better luck next time." She saw the small print that said, "Sorry for the inconvenience", but this wasn't much of a solace. A fellow traveller standing alongside beat her to it when he said, "Couldn't they think of some kind of alternative? This is the last time I fly with these guys."

This senior executive immediately thought about writing or calling the airline's CEO. She drafted the message in her mind as she trudged off toward her gate: *My expectation of friendly service was not met today. In fact, you delivered the opposite. Perhaps leadership should wonder why those in charge of renovating the lounge so flagrantly disregarded the customer. Closing the lounge without any recourse for your executive customers, your bread and butter, for heaven's sake? After all, sir, this is where the rubber meets the road.*

Imagining writing the letter made her feel better. She went on, *What if this was not an isolated event? What if throughout the rank and file, this is how things are done; how your people treat each other as well as the customer? How can you possibly expect your people to deliver on your promises? Certainly, as CEO, your goal must be to gain, not lose, customers. I know of two that you have lost today.*

By the time our travel-weary executive had fastened her seat belt, she had cooled down. In fact, in rehashing the last thoughts of her com-

> You create the brand because of how you perform. How you perform stems from the culture and what's expected; what people deliver.
>
> Paul Preston,
> Chairman,
> McDonald's UK

plaint, her complaint drifted away from scolding the airline to looking at herself and her own company. Hers was a big insurance company with nearly 30,000 employees. What if her customers had something to complain about? Her brand image was sensitive, reliable, resourceful… expedient. Her company cared when the going got tough and promised to settle claims quickly. Were those promises being delivered in the nitty-gritty, day-to-day decisions her people made, she wondered. If they were not, were customers not complaining, but just going away?

By the time the plane reached cruising altitude, she had made a note to update her company's culture audit, to take a look and see if her organisation was delivering down to the bone on what the company brand promised.

THE GOOD TRIP

In the end, the senior executive in our story did take her business elsewhere: She recently booked a flight with Virgin Atlantic—the airline whose brand image promises *the* most atypical and pleasurable flight experience you will ever have. At Virgin, upper-class customers enjoy remote check-in service and free massages and haircuts in the lounge. So of course, when our CEO arrived at the airport, she was expecting all of Virgin's highly touted services. Instead, she was

Pizza is a power brand. You have a unique emotional connection to the customer, and to keep that connection: you've got to build a culture. Your organisation and your people have to communicate to the customers those same values that you are advertising. Over time, it wears on the brand. You want to have an organisation that is a mirror-image of what you are saying in your advertising.

Tim Pulido,
Regional VP Sales & Marketing,
Frito-Lay Europe, Africa, Md East

handed a letter from Richard Branson, Virgin's chairman. It said, "We have closed our lounge for remodelling. I am sorry for the inconvenience. But we have worked out an arrangement with Japan Airlines so that you can use their lounge, which is right across the hall. With my apologies for the inconvenience, please accept 10,000 frequent flyer miles."

Well, what a difference! Odd luck to have lounge problems again, but this time the senior executive was delighted, rather than upset. Because the airline could not meet her expectations, they exceeded them! Not only did the chairman himself apologise, they also offered alternate accommodations and a reward for her patience. The result is pretty obvious: This passenger will fly with Virgin Atlantic Airlines every chance she gets, and with the other one only when there is absolutely no other choice.

When brand expectations and culture clash, the effects can devastate business. When brand and culture *match*, the effects can devastate the competition.

BRAND GETS THE CUSTOMER'S ATTENTION

Brand has evolved from drawing attention to the product to drawing attention to the company. It was once the way we differentiated our laundry

There's two airlines you can compare and contrast on brand advertising, and it just hits you between the eyes. I won't mention their names, but there is a UK airline that when you are in an interaction with them, the people enjoy working for the airline. They understand that their job is to make life easy for the customer. Any problem you present to them becomes their problem to solve. There is another major airline that is exactly the opposite—the job of the employee is to put up as many barriers as possible to the customer.

Mark Pabst,
President & COO,
St. Paul International Insurance
Company Limited

soap from the others. Advertising image-makers created a logo and slogan that represented our product. These were the vehicles to drive the product into the minds and hands of the consumer. The goal was to create something memorable, to make "our" product distinctive enough people would remember it and choose it over the plethora of competing products. Of all the others offered in the marketplace, our product caught the eye because the brand image evoked a certain set of feelings—security, confidence in quality, excellence, excitement over something new and innovative. Branding began with focus on the product.

Since those early days, brand has evolved into a large-scale, complex communication process that can add value to the corporation. A successful brand draws new customers. Take Virgin, for example. When Virgin puts it's brand on a product or service—an airline, financial service, music store, bridal service, it delivers an emotional power and communicates a definite set of positive messages to the consumer. Anyone selling Virgin products or services will initially sell more because of the value consumers associate with the brand.

Over and above the product is the added value of a brand the consumer has come to associate with a certain set of standards they can count on. For Virgin, the standards are innovation, service, and positive experience. For Pepsi,

I do feel that a different set of leadership skills will be needed in the future. Leaders must become far more responsive to customers and have greater consumer insights across cultures and languages than they have had before. It's an environment where they can't tolerate, nor should they, this slow moving, bureaucratic superstructure which was built to sustain and defend.

Tim Pulido,
Regional VP Sales & Marketing,
Frito-Lay Europe, Africa, Md East

When you see a Golden Arches in London or Paris of Frankfurt, it needs to speak to the same thing: that you are going to get a reliable experience in the quality of food, the level of service, the cleanliness of the store, and the value that you perceive is still a good deal. Quality, Service, Cleanliness and Value (QSCV) is the culture we have tried to put forward. So getting a culture that is harmonised across the customer-facing piece of the business is a key to winning in this market, as it becomes more harmonised and more common. Brand and culture connect....

Paul Preston,
Chairman,
McDonald's UK

it is fresh, young, daring, new, and alive. For Coke, it is classic, stable, guaranteed high-quality everywhere you go. For McDonald's, it is quality, service, cleanliness, and value no matter where you are in the world—be it Portland, Paris, or Puerto Vallarta.

Brand has evolved from being the image that differentiates a product's effectiveness to the image that differentiates a corporation's vision, goals and effective presence in the world. Today, branding tells us that if we go to this particular store or travel with *this* airline or buy *this* car, we are going to have a more satisfying experience than we would with the competition. Brand tells the customer, "This is who we are."

CULTURE KEEPS THE CUSTOMER COMING BACK

If we experience less than branding has led us to expect, disappointment sets in like a bad cold. And, because of the vast array of competitors from which to choose, most of us don't return to the source of disappointment; we go elsewhere, looking for products and services from a company that will fulfill our expectations. Yet, it's not enough to merely meet customer's expectations to win and keep loyal customers; companies must exceed expectations.

One of our consultants, Lyndon Williams,

had been travelling in the States and was on his way back to London when his passport and ticket were stolen. He went to the Virgin ticket counter and explained his predicament. He ended with, "I don't know what to do. I need help."

Well, help they did. Not only did they sort it all out for him, they gave him an upgrade from coach into business class. Behold the value of delivering beyond expectations! Don't you know he was relieved and very pleased? Don't you know he told a hundred people about his positive experience?

Similarly, when the work environment meets or exceeds employees' expectations, they are more empowered and motivated. In 1994, the *Harvard Business Review* (*HBR*) published a study that examined the chain-effect of having happy employees by working backward from the desired outcome. Profit, it said, is stimulated in great part by customer loyalty, which drives customer satisfaction, which is dictated by the value of services the customer receives. Value of services is the golden link in the chain. Who creates it? Satisfied, loyal, productive employees. What creates productive, empowered, motivated, caring, employees? High-quality support services and policies. If leadership enables employees to deliver results to the customer, then those satisfied employees will deliver the culture that delivers the kind of service expected from the brand

IBM had a very strong culture, but you've got to remember that IBM had a culture stamped on it by Tom Watson, Sr. and Tom Watson, Jr., both of whom were admirable people in their way, but left an indelible mark on the organisation. So when you asked people what they did, they would say "Well, I'm an IBMr." They wouldn't say, "I'm a financial analyst working for IBM."

John Steele,
Group Personnel Director,
BT plc

advertising. It's as simple and direct as that.

It makes eminent old-fashioned common sense: Employee satisfaction and loyalty lead to customer satisfaction and loyalty. When this is the case, in any company the financial outcome can be astounding. In the same *HBR* issue in 1994, authors Reichheld and Sasser measured the effect customer loyalty has on profit. They found that a mere 5 percent increase in customer loyalty can increase profit from 25 percent to 85 percent.

A case in point: By 1997, Sears had already been hard at work for a couple of years to change its culture to support the turnaround success it had forged in the early 90s. It was vital that the entire organisation deliver the brand image, "Come see the softer side of Sears", and "This is a compelling place to shop and work." That year the retail giant measured that employee satisfaction had risen by four percent. Low and behold, they found that customer satisfaction had risen 4 percent as well. four percent seems too miniscule to mention, right? But according to a 1998 *HBR* article on Sears, that four percent improvement in customer satisfaction translated into more than $200 million in additional revenue over a twelve-month period. Those extra millions increased Sears' market capitalisation by nearly one-quarter of a billion dollars. The key—Sears' managers and employees worked together, one-on-one with customers, to achieve that created value.

> The values of Carlsberg are our people, our know-how and then our Carlsberg brand. Because you should behave just as you are doing when you are visiting a good friend. You are delivering to a good friend. When you are drinking a Carlsberg beer you should have the same feeling as when you are visiting a good friend.
>
> *Flemming Lindeløv,*
> *President & CEO*
> *Carlsberg A/S*

"CULTURE IS BRAND" IS
THE BOTTOM LINE

The brand of the company: its external image, always raises expectations in the customer's mind. If the image mirrors the company culture, then the brand creates a positive experience for the customer. If the image differs from the culture, the brand is perceived as lacking integrity; merely as ad-speak manipulation playing on the customer's wishes and desires. Like a recurring dream, the image never translates into experience.

Our culture is our brand. It is what the customer actually experiences, first and last. Beyond product promises of satisfaction, it is live interaction with the organic make-up of the company: the momentary, people-to-people encounters that leave the indelible mark.

If a retail company's brand, for example, promises friendly and efficient service, then everyone in the company, from the boardroom to the broom closet, must define, promote, and demonstrate friendship and efficiency. They will be courteous, supportive, and respectful in their daily interactions with one another. Listening to and empowering each other, they will work out differences and stay open in the process. They will treat each other fairly, work for each other's success, and make sacrifices for each other when necessary. Honesty and loyalty will be the watch-

I think it is very important that there should be a sense of belonging and loyalty to the company which one serves. And that can only be created through a cohesion that develops out of common purposes and common respect, which in turn can only be developed out of dialogue.

Peter Sutherland,
Chairman & MD,
Goldman Sachs International

words as they try to move with grace and ease in their dealings with each other. They behave this way, not only because it makes them feel better, (although who can contest the value of that outcome?), but also because these behaviours create the culture that is good for business.

When customers interact with an employee, a policy, or any part of a company, the brand either comes alive or it doesn't. When it does, there is integrity: a fusion of culture and brand that produces a kind of energy that we call superior customer satisfaction.

At QVC, for example, the brand image is quality merchandise, service, and caring. Their ads build several expectations: the customer will be welcomed, treated well, given plenty of time, and offered quality products without pressure to buy. These are a terrific set of invisible goods. Who wouldn't want them? They surely get my attention. But it takes the living interaction of the employees and customers to deliver those goals; to make them visible.

This is a revolutionary concept and deserves repeating. Culture doesn't conjure or produce the brand—it *is* the brand. Until we accept this, business will continue to spend millions creating brand images that build hopes and illusions that are never realised. When those same millions are spent on both culture *and* brand, then image will become a concrete, experiential force for both the consumer and the company.

I had a presentation the other day, and they reckoned that BT's brand had a value over and above the market cap of the company, but maybe not incorporated within it, of about 5½ billion pounds; just the value of the brand, it's recognition and so on. And therefore that's a precious asset. You could damage it so easily, but you can enhance it. And if you enhance it, then it has real commercial value.

Bill Cockburn,
Managing Director,
BT UK

EXTERNAL BRANDING

The biggest obstacle to treating brand and culture as one is the habit of seeing them as two separate entities. We bring them up in a split-screen kind of way for purpose of comparison, not cohesion.

We assign branding to an advertising agency or an image-building group, many of which have not an inkling about the relationship between culture and brand. We mandate them to produce a striking image and a promise in the mind of the consumer. Yet many times, they have no real clue as to the strengths and weaknesses of our culture, and therefore no clear idea of the image that would best represent it.

To make matters worse, while the brand is being designed, management fails to reflect on how the company will deliver on this brand or on what the culture is and how the two relate? Leadership should begin by asking, "How can we design, promote, and create behaviours we want to see more of—the behaviours that will deliver on our brand promise?"

More and more companies are addressing culture issues, but not in a powerful way that relates to brand. They see culture as something they have to do to make employees feel better or to enhance teamwork. They introduce change management as a solution. But without addressing the entire culture, top to bottom, first to

> To run a global firm, you should all the time try to find that balance between corporate culture and local sensitivities, and that is where culture is absolutely essential.
>
> *Dolf van den Brink,*
> *Member of the Board,*
> *ABN Amro Holding N.V.*

last, change management merely becomes another problem and not the solution. And the result is a culture totally unaffected by the external branding and entirely unable to deliver the brand promise.

British Airways, for example, has spent millions to change its external image; yet has not changed internal service. The culture is exactly as it always has been, and service to the customer is the subject of many horror stories. BA is a thriving example of change management being the problem, not the solution.

> We know we have to change because we are becoming more international, but some of the values that we have developed have stood us in good stead competitively over the past ten years. I am not persuaded that those should necessarily change.
>
> *Brian Stewart,*
> *Chief Executive,*
> *Scottish & Newcastle plc*

THE PAN-EUROPEAN CROSSROAD

As companies become pan-European and competition intensifies, branding will become the primary way to create markets and market differences. Corporate brands will cross multiple country boundaries and attempt to take vital shape, not only within different national cultures, but also within different corporate cultures. Can a company create an overarching culture to deliver consistently on the brand promise while allowing for regional and country differences?

This is what faces every pan-European business today. No matter how well-financed the business is, or how technically prepared to cross many borders, if the culture can't deliver the brand in spite of national cultural differences—

the business loses. It will not effectively compete in a pan-European or global market. The company that delivers the brand will get the consumer. For the guys who promise, and deliver on the promise, the competitive advantage is great; virtually immeasurable.

So the live question, the burning issue, so to speak, is this: If our company brand crosses multiple boundaries, how do we build a culture that will deliver our brand while allowing for national and regional cultural differences? Clearly, it is easier to deliver on national brands, but if we are trying to build a pan-European one, then we must consider which differences within national and corporate cultures will enable our company culture to deliver on our brand. We must study which differences will be obstacles, then do what it takes to change those differences into positive forces. Without recognising and creating a culture that can deliver, we will turn off more consumers than we gain.

The principle that culture and brand must mirror and reinforce one another will be core to the pan-European success stories of the 21st century. Increased competition and multiple choices for the consumer mean that the company that gets it right in pan-Europe, gets the bigger market.

Consider the findings recently published by Time Managers International. TMI, considered a European leader in learning programmes and

> The brand promise should always be somewhat ahead of the culture so it will inspire and pull people forward. But if the brand and culture don't match at all, then you will confuse the consumer and actually destroy brand value.
>
> *Jan Froeshaug,*
> *Group President and CEO,*
> *Egmont International Holding*
> *A/S*

change processes, focuses on the human factor of the organisation. After nine years of working for European clients and testing more than 60,000 people, they made discoveries that underscore the importance of addressing brand as culture, culture as brand:

❖ Eight out of ten employees in European organisations leave their hearts behind when they go to work.

❖ One in ten are secretly looking for a new job.

❖ Four are disloyal and speak of the company in negative terms.

❖ Eight are indifferent toward the company and do not feel a sense of shared responsibility for the results.

❖ Only two are proud of their company, bring their heart to work, take the initiative for improvements, are committed, *and* feel partially responsible for the company's success.

> Our brand is our culture. Our culture is our competitive edge. We have said that from day one of setting the company up. Our USP (Unique Selling Proposition) is our culture. You know why? Because when we work with a client, we merge our people with our client's people. Our people work alongside and help improve the client staff's capabilities and skills. We always focus on people first.
>
> *Christiane Wuillamie,*
> *Chairman,*
> *CWB Systems Services plc*

MAKING CHANGES

No, training is not the solution. It is too often the first consideration when it should be the last. Training employees to deliver the service the brand promises is not the road to successful branding. Such expensive and time-consuming endeavours only send the implicit message to employees that they are to blame for not being motivated enough to be customer-oriented. Training can be very discouraging to employees. Vast dollar amounts are spent in training— how to greet people, how to talk about a product, how to suggest alternative sales, and on and on. Granted, these are good skills to develop; some employees might become more motivated to give better service. But more often than not, any good tips, ideas, behaviours, or motivations engendered by the training are squelched by an existent culture that does not respect or mirror the behaviours being trained.

Let's say, for example, that we try to teach department store floor-personnel a set of behaviours that will satisfy the customer. We make it very important. There are slogans and posters, and dozens of training classes. We do role-playing, provide role models, and what do you know! The employees actually feel empowered with their new tools. They go back to the sales floor all fired up to make a difference—and then their department manager pulls them off to shelve stock. The employees have been trained to the heights, but then are treated poorly; their motivation thwarted. In fact, they are treated much worse than they have been asked to treat the customers. If the managers and senior team members do not model the behaviours they wish from employees, if the culture itself is not a practiced organism mirroring those same values and behaviours, then the existing culture will

Egmont was a very weak brand a few years ago. First, I decided we needed to build a culture: add the core values that were critical to our business success; and only after that did we begin to push the name Egmont. Now we have a culture and values we can deliver on, so it will match our brand promise.

Jan Froeshaug,
Group President and CEO,
Egmont International Holding
A/S

extinguish in the blink of an eye any good behaviours learned during the trainings.

It boils down to this: **No matter how many training sessions, incentive programmes, and task forces we set up, if the company is not a great place to work, it won't be a great place for the customer either.**

If the employees are not empowered, turned on, and motivated, they will not do more for the customer. Resentful and disappointed, they will only go through the minimum of motions; passing on negative feelings and minimal results to the customer.

LEADING CHANGE

Leadership owns the dual responsibility not only to produce a positive and powerful brand image that creates expectations, but also to lead the culture in such a way that it delivers on the brand promise.

The task of leadership and management is to build a culture that is the living spirit of the brand,—through their own leadership, a clear vision, supportive policies that empower employees, role modelling, and constant communication. Most importantly, as leaders, we must see ourselves as part of the culture we want to create. If we are going to lead the culture to address its habitual behaviours, then we must

> I was running for a few years the BTR sports group, marketing sports champions like Greg Norman. So the brand image was very young, fast moving, sporty images, whereas the underlying company culture was very financially, pragmatically driven. The one didn't handicap the other. The one really strengthened the other.
>
> *Baron Paul Buysse,*
> *CEO,*
> *Vickers plc*

begin by changing our own habits and behaviours. Otherwise, full organisational change will not take place.

Back in the early 80s, the Broadway Department Stores in the western United States hired our firm to improve customer service: they were losing market share. We first interviewed the sales associates, the people on the floor. We asked them about customer service, what they could do about it, and why the scores here were so low. These staffers indicated they wanted to give better service, but that department managers were only interested in getting accurate inventory counts. Then we talked with the managers, who agreed they needed to give better service but didn't feel they had the time. "All my boss wants is for me to have an accurate inventory count at the end of the day", one of them told us, "so that the buyers can place their orders the following day. And it just so happens that the stock-taking needs to be done at peak customer hours so the buyers can phone New York with their counts."

The VP of Stores also agreed that the store needed a higher level of customer service, but felt trapped by Broadway Stores' image as a merchandising-driven organisation: they felt the buyers ran the show. At the board level, we noticed that all they spoke about in their meetings was merchandising and finance. Not one agenda item in any of their executive meetings concerned culture or customer service.

There is nothing more precious than your reputation, and therefore that brand, that reputation, must be reinforced, and what that therefore means is not just winning in the market, it's being smart as well; being sensitive to all these other pressures and taking them seriously and having a breed of people and culture that reflects that.

Bill Cockburn,
Managing Director,
BT UK

I think that consumers are a pretty forceful pressure group on businesses and consumers are not as short-term as analysts and the media! I mean they are demanding as to the immediate offer, but they are also asking—both when it comes to brand and when it comes to company names—"What long-term, intrinsic values do you carry and commit to?"

Antonia Ax:son Johnson,
Chairman,
The Axel Johnson Group

If you want a culture to match your brand, and I'm here to say that you do, then it has to begin with the CEO and proceed down through the organisation. Had the issue of culture started at the top, had it even been addressed at the top, it would have been felt through the organisation. As we'll talk about in the next chapter, organisations tend to be shadows of their leaders.

Antonia Axson Johnston, Chairman of The Axel Johnson Group, is keenly aware of how critical it is that culture deliver brand. She has built a culture that is very customer-oriented. "I like to look at the organisation from the perspective of the customer", she told us. "In so many organisation charts, the customer ends up at the bottom. But if we put him at the top, focus on what he wants, then those behaviours, qualities, and services begin to permeate the organisation."

When this happens, the organisation itself becomes those qualities: the culture is attuned to the customer and able to deliver what he or she desires and expects.

INTERNAL BRANDING

Whereas the task of the image-building firm is to devise a campaign to promote the *external* brand image of the company, it is the job of leadership to come up with a set of behavioural standards that mirror the brand—so that each person knows what to do and why. This is *Internal Branding* and it touches everyone at every level. Executive team members, management, employees—everyone is graded on these behavioural standards. Hiring profiles, too, must match the real standards we are trying to build into the company. And promotions, at least in part, ought to be based on whether one lives the brand or not. If brand and culture do not permeate one another, we succeed only in creating one-dimensional people who might get results, but may not do it in a way that can add value.

DELIVERING ON THE PROMISE "WE CARE"

If we can't deliver internally to our employees, they will not turn around and deliver to the customer. What if our brand advertising says, "We really care about our customers"? Let's say we pull a senior team away for an executive retreat and explore how to connect culture with this brand. Let's look at what behaviours we need at every level of the organisation so that we are consistently delivering internally the same thing that we are promising to customers.

To begin, we have to ask basic questions: What would care from employees really mean in terms

The employees who deliver that service to you, if they live the brand, a quality product will develop. If they don't live the brand, there is a distance between the producer and the user. And it has to be very, very commoditised and uninteresting products or services not to communicate the culture.

Per Bystedt,
Chairman,
Spray Razorfish

of everyday business behaviours? What does caring for each other look like, sound like? What would we have to do to role model and create that caring environment? How do we behave to create the set of behaviours we want to drive the organisation? How do we live *"We care"*?

WE ARE FAST AND FRIENDLY

Here's another good one. We promise *fast and friendly service*, but the culture is so restrained by bureaucratic procedures that are frequent and frustrating. Internally it is not fast nor friendly. All our employees know is that they have to file five barrels of paperwork, get twelve signatures, and wait until the next board meeting before they can ask for a new dishwasher for the restaurant, or convince bosses to consider employee hand-held computers for faster check-in at the airport.

What to do? The senior team must work out what fast and friendly behaviours look like, then work backward into the organisation: i.e., What do frontline employees have to do while working with the consumer? What are the skills and behaviours needed? What do the behaviours of their department managers need to be? What do the divisional managers need to do differently? What are the behaviours that need to be displayed by the senior team?

I feel that corporate culture is very important; that corporate culture and "brand" are inextricably linked. Take Volvo, for example: The culture is one of hard work and quality, which links positively to the brand value of quality and safety.

Jacob Wallenberg,
Chairman,
SE Banken Group

The signal then comes from the top. The leaders define it, then model it; they send the message that in this organisation, we live our brand promise.

YOU TALK WE LISTEN

Let's say the brand image is one of sensitivity: "We listen and we try to find the solution." Let's say your company is a savings and loan where customers go for advice: they want a friendly listening environment. But within the organisation, when senior managers attend executive meetings to present proposals, the executives are rude. They interrupt, they challenge the managers' assumptions, they question the integrity of data. They just plain don't listen.

The unenlightened executive will say that it's not important that leadership's behaviours match those we want our employees to exhibit. We are the financial guys here, the others are just customer service. The enlightened leader knows, by contrast, that he or she casts influence throughout the entire company culture. That listening has to begin in the boardroom. Each person in the company feels the results of the leader's behaviour. Believe it! The customer will never be treated better than we are treating each other. Never.

> We are not retail-focused in the sense that we don't go out and advertise; we work through an independent agency distribution system, through intermediaries. We have not felt it valuable to build a public perception on a broad base. But if you go talk to our distribution force globally, you get pretty consistent responses because we've hired people that subscribe to our values.
>
> *Mark Pabst,*
> *President & COO,*
> *St. Paul International Insurance*
> *Company Limited*

> I think it is quite idiotic that so many of these companies spend heavily on brand, and nothing on the internal culture.
>
> *Per Bystedt,*
> *Chairman,*
> *Spray Razorfish*

6 Shadow of the Leader

THE CAST OF INFLUENCE

The leader's personality is an unfailing presence within any organisation. This principle does not require conscious adaptation or acceptance to be true, nor is it automatically helpful or harmful. It simply *is*. As the leader casts a shadow throughout the entire company, people absorb and adopt whatever message the leader—by his or her behaviours—conveys. They do it without thinking. It is purely reflexive. The question then, is what the leader does with this huge impact.

Casting a Powerful Shadow throughout the Company

During one of our interviews with the chief executive of a European telecommunincations company, the themes of openness, trust, and a healthy flow of ideas surfaced. We could tell the

What I know is that the behaviour of the CEO is very important; sometimes more important than I realise. I remember one day in the lift I joked to a colleague about someone who I referred to as "that old man." My colleague said, "Georges, you called him that in the lift in front of him". To me it was just a joke. But my colleague said, "Never forget that coming from you, that man is never going to forget what you said." And I never forgot that because it was quite true. I can still remember some remarks made about me by people high-up. So a boss sometimes underestimates his influence. Everything he does, everything he says, is interpreted by the people around him.

Georges Jacobs, Chairman, Executive Committee, UCB S.A.

executive's wish that his people be more open and share more ideas was heartfelt. We could see he was frustrated and genuinely concerned: "If we can't get ideas to flow openly around here, how in the hell are we going to compete successfully in this crazy, Web-speed competitive, global telecoms marketplace?" he asked. "I tell people my door is always open. I want to hear their ideas. I'm looking for new ways to do things. But it's like pulling teeth. It must be this historical monopoly culture that is harder to penetrate that I thought it would be." While we agreed with him that the culture was not very open, we reminded him that over the past three years he had brought in numerous outside executives who had come from much speedier, more open cultures. Why weren't they providing new role models? He grinned and said, "I guess our culture has got to them, too!"

A week later: It's 4PM in the waiting room adjacent to the corporate boardroom. The management board meeting began at noon, and as usual, is scheduled to end at 5PM. The waiting room contains a few chairs, all occupied by senior- and mid-level managers who have been scheduled to make presentations at today's meeting. Suddenly, the door opens and a senior divisional manager and his two colleagues emerge. They have just finished their time at "the inquisition", as it is frequently called, and completed their presentation to the manage-

> I see too many times where there is just a complete miscommunication. I think that as a leader, you've got to use your ears as well as your mouth: you've got to listen.
>
> *John Taylor,*
> *Former CEO,*
> *British Nuclear Fuels plc*

ment board. Well, completed isn't exactly the right word.

"Whew, am I glad that's over!" said the divisional manager, with a somewhat flustered and caustic tone of voice. "First of all, they kept us waiting for two hours—a secretary came out just once to say it would be a little while longer. Then, when we finally get in and started our presentation, the CFO fired the first salvo. He challenged the integrity of our data and suggested our approach was flawed from the beginning. Then the technology guy started in on us. All we could do was play defence and respond to their critical question. They never even let us get to our recommendations, let alone to the second half of our presentation! Next time we do this, my boss can take the flack. I'm tired of spending weeks on a report only to be waylaid after the first two slides. I'm not bringing any more ideas to this group. Stuff it!"

The manager and his team left the waiting room still muttering about the meeting. Those waiting, who were also two hours behind schedule, looked at each other and silently hoped that a freak lightening strike would take out the entire building!

What Are You Looking at Me For?

In companies the world over, cultures are created every day based not on what leaders *say*,

> If you are arrogant and cynical as a leader, then you can be very sure that your organisation will be cynical and arrogant. And if you cannot, as a leader, accept that you can be wrong and make that statement and say, "Teach me how we should be thinking about this", then you can be sure that no one else will either.
>
> *Leif Johansson,*
> *President & CEO,*
> *Volvo AB*

The Axel Johnson Group was founded in 1873 by my great-grandfather. While our business evolution has been an obvious mirror of its times, I think there has been an even stronger element of the business being sculpted and formed by the personality of the owner and business leader. In the three previous generations, there was first the imaginative entrepreneur, then there was the visionary industrialist, and finally the internationalist who took the products manufactured in the Axel Johnson Group companies to the global markets. My role has then been to increase the speed of change in linking up with consumers in dialogue.

Antonia Ax:son Johnson,
Chairman,
The Axel Johnson Group

but on what they *do*! Leadership expert Dr. Warren Bennis puts it this way: "A leader doesn't just get the message across, the leader *is* the message." The following two charts visually display the "Shadow of the Leader" concept. Have you ever seen either of these leadership shadows?

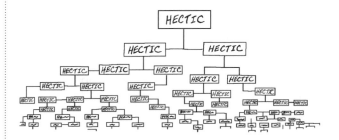

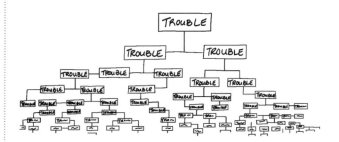

In the case above, why is the culture so closed and ideas so constrained? The answer lies in the shadow being cast by the senior team. Their behaviour in the management board meeting was not an isolated event; it reflected their individual management styles as well. They tended to react quite aggressively and in a confronta-tional manner when their own mangers brought new ideas to them. How could responsible senior leaders behave so badly, you say? Well, when we pressed them for an answer, they said they genuinely believed they were helping the company by being challenging and digging hard for the real facts. Their intention was good: The execution was atrocious!

Before we suggested the possibility, it had never dawned on them that their disrespectful, non-listening behaviours cast a dark shadow throughout the entire company of 120,000 employees. They had never even considered that they themselves created the lack of openness they said they wanted to change! Though each employee had heard through the grapevine, at one time or another, about "the inquisition," the senior team was clueless and dumbfounded when they heard the term.

The Gulf Crisis

In European business today, there is a deep gulf between the senior board and everybody else. Bridging it will do no less than make or break our ability to transform our corporations into effective competitors in the global market-place. Healing the "gulf crisis" is a critical chal-lenge facing companies at the start of the new millennium.

The first thing about lead-ership is, you've got to be yourself. The absolute key to success is to be you. If you're not you, then there's a little maggot in the back of the brain that says, "I don't buy this guy."

Bob Lawson,
CEO,
Electrocomponents plc

The team that doubled our profitability had all been in Meridian for more than seven years, and yet this business had gone backwards for seven years. So what I did there was help them change their thinking. They were a bit nervous—they were all given new jobs, very often in areas that they had criticized for many years. They are now running it. It changes the leadership dynamics in terms of getting the team to think differently.

Charles Allen,
CEO,
Granada Group plc

Communication has to flow, or not much else will—except perhaps negativity, fear, and resistance. And communication isn't just talk. What's more, in the new business environment, idea exchange and understanding must flow at *Web speed*, just like all the other information out there.

The shadow of the leader, in speeded-up 21st century Europe, must cast itself more positively, profoundly, and multidimensionally than ever before because it will not be possible to address verbally and instantly all the areas that require leadership in the new environment: The leader's influence must cross traditional boundaries and enter the Information Age.

Leaders in the new century must be influential and multidimensional enough to engender leadership down through the organisation. And that cannot be done in memo or meeting form, or by issuing directives. Mending communication gaps and restoring leadership accountability will make the difference between failure in business and success.

21ST CENTURY VID-KID

Most adults have a hell of a time with those computer games, but kids are absolute wizards at them. Kids have multidimensional vision—in fact, they have *everything* it takes to win at these games. They have peripheral, forward, and spatial vision, as well as speed and flexibility. Those skills provide them with the ability to keep up with—and even stay ahead of—the scenes moving all at once, in several directions. They understand how and where the different levels connect and interrelate.

The varieties of skill required for leadership in the 21st century are comparable. The leader must have functional, strategic, and leadership skills. To these we must add another dimension: the ability to empower others to lead, not just to manage. Teams and teamwork are essential to the new environment.

IF IT'S GOOD ENOUGH
FOR MY PRESIDENT...

Not long ago, I consulted for an aerospace firm. When I met with the president, he was standing behind a specially designed desk, in fact, an exact replica of Thomas Jefferson's desk. "You don't mind if I stand, do you?" he asked. "I have a bad back. I actually kind of like working this way." I was mildly surprised and interested, but I did not take too much notice of it. Later, when I toured the company and met the senior staff, four of those executives had stand-up desks, too! *Either there's a bad-back epidemic in the aerospace industry,* I

It is like driving a Ferrari at a self-imposed 40 mph when a Ferrari is capable of doing 150 mph. We have culturally inbuilt braking systems, and I think we have got to encourage people to do a bit more speeding without tickets. The job of the leader is genuinely to encourage and to move, and to recognise that there is much less risk in taking that chance than traditionally might have been assumed. And even if there are a few failures, learn from them.

Bill Cockburn,
Managing Director,
BT UK

thought, *or this was living proof of the "Shadow of the Leader" principle.*

Of course it was the "Shadow of the Leader." This example represents the kind of influence that happens in every arena, mostly in more subtle ways. Just notice, sometime. If the top guy smokes a Macanudo three times a day (or more!), bet the senior team does as well. If the senior group drinks a lot, or plays golf in the early morning, or runs, not only is it likely the chief does to, but so do folks throughout the organisation.

The principle is simple: The behaviours modelled at the top will be prevalent throughout the organisation. A leader who arrives late can have the most strictly worded tardiness policy ever devised, but his people won't respect punctuality.

> I have absolutely no doubt in my mind that the senior team has to be aligned to get maximum performance.
>
> *Helen Alexander,*
> *CEO,*
> *The Economist Group*

Not too long ago, I attended a large corporate event at the invitation of the CEO. It was an evening affair, with dinner and a guest speaker, capping-off two days of business meetings. The mood was festive; the guest speaker actually a comedian. The lights dimmed, the curtain opened, and the guest speaker appeared. What ensued over the next five minutes was the greatest example of how a leader can cast a shadow over an entire corporation that I have ever seen.

When the comedian opened up with the first of a string of steadily more ribald and off-colour jokes, the laughter was guarded. Everyone had heard the CEO's speech a few hours earlier about the importance of the company's corporate values, trust, respect for the individual, high ethical and moral principles and caring. As the comedian continued, people cast nervous glances a the CEO. People were unsure whether to laugh or not. The act was funny, sort of, but it just really didn't feel right for this company. Maybe in Las Vegas, but here?

At the end of the third joke, when the comedian's language was becoming more suitable for a bar than a business meeting, the CEO stood up, walked up on stage, took the microphone away from the comedian, shook his hand and firmly stated: "Thank you, but your presentation is over. You will receive your fee. You are free to leave now." There was not a whisper or a cough in the entire ballroom. Then the CEO spoke. "I would like to personally apologise for the past few minutes", he said. "The act did not match our values and I believe very strongly in our values and our culture. Innuendoes, crude jokes, and raunchy humour are the opposite of our values of respect, trust, and care for each other. I firmly believe our culture is what will help us win in the marketplace and make this company a great place to work. And I won't sacrifice our values for an evening of jokes. Why don't we enjoy each others' company and finish our dinner with the people we care about, each other."

By the next day, word was all over the company that the CEO took seriously the culture's values. The story became one of the under-

"People will sometimes believe what you say; they will always believe what you do."—That saying has been hanging on my door for a long time.

Kees Storm,
Chairman, Executive Board,
Aegon N.V.

ground messages that old-timers told to new employees about the culture. This is a powerful example of casting a leadership shadow. It is behaviour that people really follow, not words. It is not a question of influencing or not; rather, it is a question of leadership. The shadow exists. We need to be conscious of how our shadow is creating our culture.

Often the shadow of the leader is quite visible, even to outsiders. Consider Microsoft. Bill Gates *and* his company are seen as innovative, competitive—even aggressive. Wal-Mart's friendly customer-orientation, combined with its fanatical attention to costs, is deemed a direct reflection of the personality of its founder, the late Sam Walton.

WALKING… AWAY FROM SLUMPING MORALE

Like a parent raising children, the corporate leader must model desired behaviour in order for his or her people to adapt it. "Do what I say, not what I do" has never worked as a paradigm of leadership—or parenting, for that matter. No one ever buys it, nor will they. Nor *should* they. Modelling involves values in action: a live illustration not only of what the desired behaviour looks like, but of why it works and why it is valuable. Human beings possess the capacity for

> I use visits to ensure our communications are working. It's about ensuring your own managers are out there leading as well, and the key issue for me is leading genuinely, by example. What they see you doing, they start doing. It's simple things; for example, when I am out in restaurants I will taste the food, and when I'm out in the hotels I will actually go and test the product.
>
> *Charles Allen,*
> *CEO,*
> *Granada Group plc*

understanding that not only separates them from the rest of the animal kingdom, but requires that the leadership bar be raised in all of us, throughout our organisations.

In our experience, in the worst cases of slumping morale, the culprit is always leaders not walking the talk. This can obviously take an infinite number of forms. Some of the more basic are:

❖ Expenses and salaries are being cut everywhere in the organisation except on the top tier, where executive perks are thriving displays of conspicuous consumption;

❖ Teamwork is touted as a core value for the company, yet the senior team makes it plain they don't really like each other and don't work well together;

❖ The organisation asks people to change in major ways, but the leaders are not modelling the change;

❖ Personal development is promoted as a way to attract new talent, yet middle managers haven't had a face-to-face performance review with their boss in years.

Our years of leadership consulting work have proven, beyond a doubt, that unless a senior team formally, eagerly, and actively engages in whatever is being asked of everyone in the organisation—be it training, merger-related

A lot of people in leadership jobs don't understand the extent to which people will take you as a model. That is true—and that is where we educate CEOs a bit more on their responsibilities, because they are enormous.

Georges Jacobs,
Chairman, Executive Committee,
UCB S.A.

change management, any culture-shaping effort—the changes don't work.

CEOs and senior teams must confront behaviour issues head-on, otherwise meetings and directives become communications fiascos. Poor modelling at the top shows up in the ranks perhaps most obviously in the ways people communicate, or seem to. Some of these are:

❖ *Skewed-View Syndrome.* Everyone knows members of the senior team disagree on an issue, even though management presents a consensual viewpoint in memos.
❖ *E-Hall Talk.* People are quiet at the meetings and the real discussions take place afterward, in the hall, at lunch, on e-mail.
❖ *Triangle Speak.* "A" tells "B" what "C" needs to be doing, but utters nary a direct syllable to "C" himself.
❖ *The Silent Stalker*, a.k.a., *the Pocket Veto.* No one says so directly, but they have no intention of carrying out new plans, or working toward newly defined goals.
❖ *007 Cipher*, a.k.a., *the Hidden Agenda.* What is said bears little resemblance to what is meant. People keep real concerns to themselves out of fear or some other discomfort that prevents major issues from being raised directly.

Children have never been very good at listening to their elders, but they have never failed to imitate them.

James Baldwin, American Author

Worst Case Scenario

The worst manifestation of slumping morale can't even make the list, because it is when people cease to try at all; when they are too discouraged or unmotivated to attempt even indirect communication.

I spoke with a middle-manager who, after several years with a large company, only occasionally would venture down the senior team's hall with a suggestion. Each time she did, she met with frustration: The executives were either unresponsive, unsure of what she meant, or uncomfortable with the ideas being suggested.

Returning from the senior hall—secretly dubbed by the ranks "The Trellis" for the flourishing plant life it housed—she would joke with colleagues that she didn't know whether to hazard making further suggestions or simply beat her head against the nearest brick wall. After all, the results would be the same. Her co-workers would chuckle and nod, knowingly.

Morale was abysmal. Of the few long-term staffers in the company, most felt that a core group of front-line employees kept the entire ship afloat while the rest watched talented operations managers and sales executives leave, one after the other. Even the hardworking front-liners could not keep the company from an eventual steep decline in profits that preceded an even

You are in a goldfish bowl, and as a leader and a manager you will not be able to just rely on your authority to establish your credibility. Your credibility will be on your actions, your value added, and people will be looking for that inspiration, that buzz, that excitement.

Bill Cockburn,
Managing Director,
BT UK

The real management challenge is actually trying to attract and retain high-competency, self-sufficient individuals. On the other hand, you must get them to align. That's a critical role of the CEO; to manage that dynamic.

Mike Grabiner,
CEO, Energis

larger exodus of core employees; and ultimately a hostile takeover.

Build It and They Will Play

Building an aligned leadership team is crucial to the survival and success of an organisation. These are not just recruited; they are cultivated —carefully. Developing such teams requires the commitment of everyone, most importantly the senior team. A valuable process is to hold an off-site senior executive workshop on a yearly basis to work out obstacles and learn to practice the leadership skill of modelling. Out of such seminars come not only ideas, but tangible progress toward casting a more conscious, and positive, shadow. Most management teams find they must create a pact that involves several components, including a commitment to:

❖ Address any and all issues and concerns directly with each other, rather than with *any* third party;
❖ Represent a unified team to the organisation—formally and informally;
❖ Be supportive of each other at all times, not just when in the same room;
❖ Engage in healthy debate, work to reach alignment, and commit to supporting the group decision once it is reached.

DO AS I DO, AND SO WILL I

Leaders we interviewed were quite concerned about their effect on the company and think about it quite a bit. In fact, more and more executives are choosing to adopt solid leadership behaviour. Each day provides a thousand small opportunities to lead.

Leaders who will survive in the new environment recognise the importance of Distributed Leadership as a means of casting a beneficial and profitable shadow. As Chapter 3 of this book established, leadership has to extend further down the organisation. Traditional wisdom maintained that management had to extend down the organisation, but not *leadership*. Today, all people in the company must be prepared to commit acts of leadership, whether they are middle management, sales, or human resources people.

Make Chaos Your Friend

One of the CEOs we interviewed reminded us to consider Chaos Theory in talking about developing leadership throughout the organisation. Chaotic systems are unpredictable because they are sensitive to their starting conditions. Leaders can take steps, however, to build in to their "starting conditions" some rules that can add stability, if not predictability. A few of these

My simple philosophy is, nobody comes to work to screw up. 90,000 people working for Granada didn't wake up this morning and think, I will go in and screw up today. But people do screw up sometimes, mostly because we, as leaders, are not being clear on exactly what we want. None of us can be a one-man band, and the key part of my job is to communicate clearly, and to coach and develop people.

Charles Allen,
CEO,
Granada Group plc

I think Europe has certain visionary, charismatic leaders who at the same time are good with the nuts and bolts of the business. We are going to need more of these. Meanwhile, competition will just force us to get the right people for the job.

Lode Beckers,
Chairman,
Lobo n.v.

rules are essential to the development of 21st century leadership:

❖ The shadow of the leader is critical. The leader must cast a positive shadow;

❖ The sooner each individual develops leadership qualities, the better leader he or she will eventually become;

❖ Leadership at the top, from here on out, will involve more *influence* on the corporation and less *control* of it. Dictatorial rule is a thing of the past;

❖ Finally, there will continue to be the concept of "the leader" at the top of big organisations. "The leader" is the very element of the organisation that will yield the flexibility to change fast enough to play in the global game. The concept of "Distributed Leadership", on the other hand, will keep the environment current; another key to playing globally.

The toughest challenge for people at the top may very well be the task of Distributed Leadership. To some it will feel like relinquishing control. Yet, in fact, Distributed Leadership *sustains* the top position of the leader. Understanding the importance of the leader's influence, and adopting necessary behaviours, will be the very passage to the multidimensionality required of the 21st century leader. The vastness of the new environment must be shared. Leaders who cast the appropriate shadow will create cultures that allow their organisations to thrive.

Walking the "Right" Talk

Leaders have to "walk the talk," but what is it that they are saying? If the CEO works seventy hours a week and is on his third marriage, does anyone really want to emulate him? What about the pace in the new environment? To cast a positive influence, must the leader work faster and longer? Should he or she read more, and be aware of every detail of day-to-day operations?

On the contrary, what the doctor orders to attain *Web-speed* leadership skill... is *Balance of Life*, the focus of our discussion in Chapter 7.

You have to lead by example. Help your colleagues. Keep them involved. It's not about salary; it's about confidence.

Tom Hedelius,
Chairman,
Svenska Handelsbanken

7 Balance of Life

GETTING TO THE POINT

I sat down one day to interview a CEO for this book and the first thing I noticed was how tired he looked. Even though he had put his "game face" on as all good executives do, anyone who has worked with senior executives would have recognised the chronic fatigue evident on his face. He was not just tired that day. Over time he had worn thin, both physically and mentally. Since personal well-being was an issue on my list, I brought it up first.

" HI, MRS. GALLAGHER? I'M DAN. YOUR HUSBAND FORGOT TO PENCIL YOU IN FOR THIS EVENING SO I'M COVERING FOR HIM. WHAT'S FOR DINNER? I'M STARVED... "

Drawing by P. Kleba; © 1994 SDLCG © 1994 Senn-Delaney Leadership Consulting Group Inc.

> Balance comes by having outside interests that ensure social dialogue that is not exclusively within the area of business. Balance comes when we can carve-out time for reflection. Such time is absolutely necessary to be able to make proper decisions. I think every manager should allot time everyday that is empty time—for reflection, emergencies, whatever.
>
> *Peter Sutherland,*
> *Chairman & MD,*
> *Goldman Sachs International*

> Personal balance in life is an absolutely fundamental issue. Many of us don't talk about it because we are not comfortable talking about it. I think there is a view that if you talk about it, maybe you are weak.
>
> *John Steele,*
> *Group Personnel Director, BT plc*

You have to create an environment where peoples' minds are healthy, because in my personal experience, someone working twelve- or fourteen-hour days, seven days a week, is not more productive than someone working ten hours a day, five days a week.

Christiane Wuillamie,
Chairman,
CWB Systems Services plc

Everybody says, "I don't have the time to exercise." I say that's nonsense. I run from 6:30 to 7:30 in the morning, three to four times a week, so I feel fit. And my doctor tells me I am. Everybody tells me "I don't have the time, I travel too much." I travel more than almost anyone who says that does, and my response is—it's nonsense. You can have your shoes with you in your suitcase and you can run wherever you are. If you want to be the CEO of a company, you'd better be in good shape. You owe it to the organisation.

Kees Storm,
Chairman, Executive Board,
Aegon N.V.

Now, I've noticed this is a subject many executives are uncomfortable with, but this CEO was thrilled to talk about it. Apparently he had just recently made a revelatory assessment of himself: "I took a good look at my life the other day", he said, "and I saw what was missing".

I barely had time to ask, "What?" when he fired back, "…my kids, my wife, and the wisdom I used to have in dealing with people and problems".

"You know", he went on, " I just cannot get on another airplane, not until I figure this thing out. I am so out of balance that I can't ignore the symptoms any more. I don't remember conversations. My head is cluttered. I've been dropping the ball more. I've left important papers behind—once in a cab, recently in a hotel room. Even with a reminder, I forgot my wife's birthday. I'm amazed I have on matching socks these days." He looked down and was relieved to see two of the same.

"I know I'm off balance", he said, "because I don't have the essential things that keep me in balance, the things that are most important to me. As it stands now, I don't see my kids unless I squeeze in some brief interactions between air flights, or phone calls and e-mail on the weekends. I don't know when my wife and I last took a walk, read the paper together, or had an open-ended conversation at the kitchen table. And exercise— I'm lucky if I get in one physical workout a week."

Quality time, "just a little while alone to mull

things over", he told me, had become a thing of the past.

"I used to count on the few hours of plane travel", he said, " for quiet thought. But nowadays, every time-crunched executive, including myself, is up there in the jet stream, habitually using the airplane as an office." Instead of time for quiet reflection, he had to use the time for the nuts and bolts planning and preparation he didn't have time to do on the ground.

"What I see is that I have lost touch with what is important to me, and I'm not being effective as a result. I end up so worried about my home life, about my own health, and about not having enough time to think, that I can't gain perspective on issues. The quality of my thinking is definitely declining. Clarity is rare and I no longer trust the wisdom of my decisions."

He told me how his dealings with colleagues and customers had become less productive, too, because he wasn't nearly as capable when he was agitated or stressed. "I fumble around with my own ideas and words", he said, "while totally missing the little tell-all subtleties of behaviour of those who are trying to communicate with me. I don't have patience or tolerance, and I certainly don't have the compassion that I would if I were in a more balanced state of well-being."

It was all too clear, as we continued the interview, that this CEO was at a terrific crisis point—

I work out three days a week. It's to the point where I ask my secretary to call ahead and make sure the hotel I'm staying at has got a gym. It gives me greater energy and more fuel, shall we say, to confront the challenges that are out there.

Tim Pulido,
Regional VP Sales & Marketing,
Frito-Lay Europe, Africa, Md East

One absolute fundamental is that I am religious about is my holidays. And to help guard my time, I try not to let the phone, PC, and e-mail get in the way. Secondly, the only thing that keeps me going is having weekends at home. Even if I only arrive home on Saturday morning from wherever, I can still spend thirty-six hours recharging my batteries with my wife and kids. It's my time to just try being a sensible guy for a change, instead of a mad executive!

Robert Binney,
Managing Director,
Citibank N.A.

I mean, if I don't run in the morning, I don't feel right. It is so much a part of my make-up that I go out. And I don't spend a lot of time thinking about business when I run. I spend a lot of time running and thinking about running when I am doing it. What run am I going to run? How many miles am I going to go? What kind of time am I pacing my running at? I think that it just helps keep the mind and the body working to be more effective during the course of the day.

Dale Gallagher,
VP Operations,
Frito-Lay Europe

I have a son from my first marriage, and I can see the way he is to his children compared to how I was to him. I have a very close relationship with him but that came late in life. But I missed him growing up. I sometimes have to encourage people to take their vacations. I think the younger generation is wanting more balance because they have seen their parents' lives being one long working life.

Vagn Holck Andersen,
Chairman,
Interdan A/S

one that offered great opportunity. He was just awakening to the fact that he had lost his way, that he had given up his own equilibrium in favour of some notion of business success. As part of the same wake up call, he also knew that it was up to him; that he was accountable for both the lack and the return of balance in his life. "I'm not getting on another airplane" he said, "until I figure this thing out".

GETTING TO THE POINT OF BALANCE

Every human being is more productive when in a balanced state of physical and psychological well-being. That is the principle of Balance of Life in a nutshell.

For the business leader in particular, personal balance results in capabilities that are highly valued these days—perspective, clear thinking, and good ideas. Having time and energy for all that is important to us in life makes us relaxed, rested, flexible, and optimistic. Our minds remain open and uncluttered so that ideas can bubble up from their buried places. To put it another way, good ideas can only come to us when our anxiety, fatigue, and agitation are out of the way. If we live in a balanced way with all our creative channels open, then not only can ideas flow, but also we experience the added value of wisdom and insight which tend to rise out of quiet, reflective moments.

Every leader must make personal health and balance a priority. Even though balance is a tricky thing to achieve and is different for everybody, the CEO must make it a priority, or it won't happen. His or her effectiveness and the health and effectiveness of everyone in the organisation depends on it. When the leader models personal health and balance, then those around him or her will do the same.

Does the Hinge Squeak? The Wheel Wobble? Am I out of Whack?

What happens most often is we get into a kind of blind state where we think we're effective, but we aren't. We cruise along on auto-pilot and don't pick up on early indicators that something is wrong. The indicators, to be sure, are always there. As leaders, we have to train ourselves to become aware of and recognise them early.

If I drive my car everyday, for example, and one tyre is a little off-balance, I might not pay much attention to it. Gradually, as time goes by, I barely notice that little wobble while driving. Then comes the day when I'm driving at high speed and a violent vibration nearly shakes the car out of control. I almost drive off the road. By then I know that to keep driving could do serious damage to the car, to me, and/or to others.

In the same way, our fast-paced business world needs balanced leaders, not leaders who

I am finding that I often must call a "time out." Some misread it as indecisive, but "I'll get back to you tomorrow" buys valuable time to weigh the compelling arguments being made from different constituencies. Time is often necessary to confirm integrity of facts as our systems are not sufficiently integrated.

I also make it a rule not to make critical decisions when jet lagged.

Bill McLaughlin,
Former President & CEO,
Frito-Lay Europe

I'm a devout Roman Catholic and I still like to make a retreat periodically. I think having time to reflect on what you are doing and how you are doing it and what's important is critical.

Rob Amen,
President,
International Paper Europe S.A.

are a little wobbly and getting worse with every tick of the clock. We need leaders who are healthy, well rested, and thoughtful to stay the course, with power and effectiveness.

Consider a well-tuned athlete. Each time she prepares to work out, the athlete checks into her physical state. The left calf is feeling tight; the ankle is stiff. She does preparatory stretches or rotations to loosen the calf and ankle. This is how she gets an efficient workout and avoids injury.

There is no magic formula for balance. It is an individual state requiring an individual solution. But the ways to check-in for indicators of balance or imbalance are the same for everyone. We must begin with how we are *feeling*, not how are we *doing*. Feelings are the barometer of our thoughts. They are the external manifestation of our thoughts. They tell us how we are doing mentally, physically, and emotionally. Take the time every day to check in:

❖ *How am I feeling? Am I rested or exhausted?*
❖ *How am I mentally? Am I optimistic or pessimistic, positive or negative about people, places, and things?*
❖ *How am I emotionally? Am I anxious or secure, angry, glad, or sad?*

Comparing current feelings to healthy, well-balanced ones can produce a self-awareness and

---

When I went into the role, I hardly had any holiday in that first year; which is terribly unhealthy and wrong. Everybody needs to have his or her holidays. I tend to work quite long hours and I am coming around to the train of thought that if you can't do your job in working hours, then you shouldn't be doing the job. But it is a cultural thing, and I don't lead very well in that regard because I am very often here quite late. But as I am becoming more experienced, and becoming more efficient with my management team, I think that I am achieving better results in terms of a balance for my own life.

Sarah Williams,
CEO,
Globecast Northern Europe Ltd

I don't think we prepare the younger managers to really understand the demands that can be placed upon them— and the sacrifices. I try to get to the gym two to three days a week and that's about the only time I have for myself. And I've now talked my wife into to coming to the gym, so at least it is something we do together as well.

Rob Amen,
President,
International Paper Europe S.A.

quick personal assessment and a recognition, *Boy, I am really off-balance here, not myself at all!*

Home life is where success-driven people suffer first from being out of balance. The drive to accomplish takes on a greedy life of its own that overshadows family life. This can have disastrous consequences—even for those motivated young executives able to go all day and all night without so much as a yawn. Home should be the first place all business leaders look for balance-alarm indicators. Physically perhaps, they are resilient; but emotionally, spiritually, and mentally they are rapidly depleting their own psychic bank accounts.

Next, seek feedback on a regular basis. Sources are all around us. We must ask our spouses, our children, our friends, our colleagues: "Do you think I am being effective here? What could I do to be more effective? Is there something you see that I don't see?" Then we have to be willing to hear what they're going to tell us.

Sometimes feedback is difficult to take in. With luck it won't have to be as rattling a wake up call as, "I'm leaving you. I'm taking the kids, goodbye." Or, its physical equivalent, a heart attack. However, even non-cataclysmic, honest, and helpful responses can be difficult to hear: "(Such and such) is happening and we need to talk. You are not firing on all cylinders."

Personal balance in the organisation is a tough issue, because we're talking about adults whom you assume know what they are doing. So, it's hard to interfere when the signs (of being out of balance) are there. Everyone goes for a medical exam once a year and we have people who can help, so we have a lot of support. And ultimately I will plead, cajole, reason or do a combination to help.

Jim Wadia,
Worldwide Managing Partner,
Arthur Andersen

I know there are some executives who feel that their every waking hour belongs to the company. But I am not willing to work for a company where that is the case. We've got to get some balance. We are not on this earth just to do whatever we have to do for our business lives. Our personal lives round us out and satisfy us like nothing else, not even our business life, can.

Robert Binney,
Managing Director,
Citibank N.A.

LET'S FIGURE IT OUT NOW! THIS IS FAR TOO IMPORTANT TO TAKE SERIOUSLY!

OK, fine, but what's a leader to do when confronted with the eighteen-hour day full of business demands? How did the CEO in our opening story figure it out?

First, it's simple. Second, it's difficult. Third, it can be done. It sounds corny, but it takes old-fashioned discipline.

The CEO in our opening story had to make time for exercise, diet, downtime, and pleasures with his family. He had to make time for art, music, theatre, dance, sport and relationships other than business ties. From all of these things, he draws inspiration and renewal.

No one is going to *hand* him, or any busy person, extra time. The business certainly won't make time for him. The business is a living gargantuan organism with its own unending appetites and demands. Each of us has to find and make the time to have and do the things that keep us balanced and effective.

Even though balance is a personal matter, here are some do's and don'ts suggested by executives who are constantly checking in and re-balancing:

❖ Don't take your briefcase home. If you do, it will open itself and suddenly work will become the focus of time at home.

> I cannot think today of successful chief executives emerging that are not in some way multi-suit individuals.
>
> *Rupert Gavin,*
> *Chief Executive,*
> *BBC Worldwide*

> I gave up golf because my wife doesn't play, and six hours on a Saturday just takes up too much time. We spend time with each other and the family. And it gives me better balance at work as well.
>
> *Paul Preston,*
> *Chairman,*
> *McDonald's UK*

❖ Organise your time. It sounds trite, but it's vital. Some senior executives hire a driver for the morning and night rides. That way, by the time they've reached the office, they've made a dozen phone calls—the calls they would otherwise have to make at the office. Similarly, on the night ride home, they make calls to tie up loose ends. When they arrive home then, they can be there 100 percent with whoever is there or whatever is planned.

❖ Don't send or read e-mail from home. If you absolutely must, then none after 9:00 at night or before work in the morning.

❖ Don't bring work home on the weekend.

❖ Don't demand weekend work from your people. Nothing should be due on Monday morning.

❖ Workout at least three times weekly. Exercise clears the mind.

❖ Try one workout with a family member.

❖ Schedule dedicated empty time every day. Use it for quiet reflection.

❖ Book holiday time a year in advance, setting aside at least three–four weeks for the family.

In terms of how to keep perspective on events, I think it is exceedingly important to perform at least one non-executive director role. I personally do two, and I find that exceedingly heartening as it allows me to escape from the narrow perspective of Reuters and see things from the outside. It is absolutely essential for top executives to do that.

Peter Job,
CEO,
Reuters plc

First, I don't work on the weekends, and second, I do not take work home—ever. If it can't be done between Monday and Friday, or on an airplane, it will not be done. Those five days between the two weekend days is work time and the weekends are not. I'm pretty religious about that. Then, I will stay late, I will come in early, but I do not invade personal space with work.

Mark Pabst,
President & COO,
St. Paul International Insurance
Company Limited

I attach an enormous importance to Balance of Life. It is major for me as a human being. My family is tremendously important to me—my wife, my children, my brothers. Spiritual values are essential for me to have harmony in my job and in my life. Knowledge of the political and cultural world that surrounds me is very important. And then to have harmony and balance of all that is essential.

Baron Daniel Janssen, Chairman, Solvay S.A.

BE HERE NOW—YOU DON'T HAVE TO BE A GURU TO LIVE IN THE MOMENT!

When each of us looks at our lives, we can come up with specific priorities that help us maintain our balance of life. Once our time is allocated to tasks that reflect our priorities, we need only one other tool: Be Here Now. When I am Here Now I can empty my mind of all else except what I am concentrating on at the moment. We've all been in meetings with someone who isn't *here now*. He may be physically present, but mentally he's someplace else. When that someone is an executive, we can bet the meeting will be a waste of time.

Most of us have gone home in the evening, walked into the house, greeted our loved ones, sat down to dinner conversation, and all the while our minds have remained on a problem at work. Sometimes it takes two or three hours before our minds find their way home. Some nights, they never do. Such is our own case of Being There Then instead of Being Here Now.

Be Here Now is the tool that allows me to pour myself 100 percent into the present moment. When I'm in conversation with my spouse, I am 100 percent there. When I'm listening to a presentation at work, I am 100 percent there as well. This ability increases my effectiveness because I am focused and concentrated.

More gets done with less repetition, confusion, and wasted energy.

Here is a case in point; the success, failure, and success of the great tennis star, Jimmy Connors. He devoted his life to becoming the number one world champion player. To maintain that status, he had to practice continually, and did.

When Connors got married and he and his wife had a baby, he began to feel anxious and guilty for spending practice time away from his son. To alleviate those feelings, he spent more time with his son and less on the court. But then he felt guilty for not practicing. Connors pretty quickly lost his number-one ranking because he had become stuck in a kind of a limbo. He was never completely in either place—with his son or on the court—and he was in constant anxiety about it.

When Connors began to practice Be Here Now, he became 100 percent present at his court workouts—physically, mentally, and emotionally. Those sessions became much more productive. And because his workouts were productive, he felt he had more time to spend with his son. And he did. When he was with his son, he was also there 100 percent—which gave Connors and his son an experience of quality time that they had sorely missed. Eventually, as we all know, Connors regained his ranking.

I do think you've got to have a life outside the business. I am married with two children and I enjoy their company hugely. I do not believe leadership is about seven days a week, 365 days a year. It's about rejuvenation. It's about being able to come in physically and mentally up to it.

Bob Lawson,
CEO,
Electrocomponents plc

We need to think deeper than mere business skills require. We need to be philosophical thinkers. If we are not philosophical, we will never be good chief executives. I try every day to reflect on my day, and reflect on my week. I hope and believe that we do what we do in order to become better persons, to make a difference in the world and to contribute to the health of the environment.

Baron Paul Buysse,
CEO,
Vickers plc

YOU MEAN I DON'T HAVE TO
WORK EIGHTY HOURS TO SUCCEED?

There is a healthy balance between challenge and rest, between work and family, individual goals and business goals and personal dreams and career objectives. One activity needs and nurtures the other.

There is no single and set point at which all these are in balance. What makes us healthy is the process of awareness and the actions we take to continually balance them, as we do instinctively when skiing or riding a bike.

Balance is a dynamic state, and each person has to experience it for him/herself. I don't have the same standard and capability as my business partner, Larry Senn, does, for example. My point of balance is slightly different. It is not so much a question of balance as it is learning how to achieve it. Sometimes I will put in a little more on the work side than on the family side or vice-versa. But to let even a little imbalance become a habit would damage both my equilibrium and my effectiveness.

When the leader commits to living a balanced life, it becomes a value to the organisation. No one can legislate health as a priority, but if the leader gains balance, so will the individuals within the company.

If the leader is personally out of balance, driving himself too hard, for example, he will model

When you see people coming in with their heads down and the world is on top of them, you know they haven't got the balance right. This is a game, which doesn't mean to say it is frivolous. But when you are confronted with some of the more serious issues in life, you realise that even though we take this game seriously, it's not life and death. It's a huge business, but if you go at it with a sense of purpose; to have some fun, then you can do remarkably well and have a balance in life.

David Thorpe,
Vice President Global Operations
Information Solutions,
EDS

drive as the way to win in the company—and the rest of the executive team and the entire work force will mirror that. Eventually, the organisation becomes one where everyone works twice as hard as the next guy until they all burn out. The end results here are sub-optimal, to say the least.

On the other hand, if the leader is a model of balance and well-being, he will make Be Here Now and individual equilibrium important goals for the entire organisation. He will talk about personal responsibility for balance. It will be on the agenda at top-level meetings. His influence will be one of promoting and respecting individual expressions of balance.

In such an organisation, one person might be fine working fifteen hours and another might be comfortable with eight or nine. It is OK for the latter to go home, turn off the phone or computer, whatever, after eight or nine hours. There is no pressure to work beyond the balance point. If there were a pressure to spend x number of hours at work, then that person's performance and attitude might slump, which could affect the whole culture.

THE EUROPEAN ADVANTAGE

Europeans have always had a healthy regard for the restorative qualities of time away from work—holidays and weekends. They value such time

> When you're at work, be really focused, and with your family, be really 100 percent with them and they know *you're* there. And when you're at work don't be pining that you should be at the recital. Be at your work and get it done efficiently. Then go and catch the second half of the recital.
>
> *Rob Amen,*
> *President,*
> *International Paper Europe S.A.*

> I would say it is essential for a leader to be balanced, because that is how you maximize the value you add to the business. But it's tough to find and do the things that balance you. It requires discipline. My wife and I have a good deal of our social life not involved with the company. We'll go out to a Tapas Bar and just enjoy ourselves somewhere where I'm not the boss. It's a matter of deciding what's important for you and getting yourself back in check.
>
> *Paul Preston,*
> *Chairman,*
> *McDonald's UK*

I have a number of golden rules, and the first one is to have fun in life. If I don't enjoy what I am doing, I will walk away from it, because life is too short. The second rule is, when I leave the office I don't think of business. I concentrate on the things I enjoy that keep the mind fresh. And thirdly, I enjoy all the love I get from my family and friends.

Paul Buysse,
CEO,
Vickers plc

Balance in the lives of all our colleagues and employees, as represented by time for recreation, family and work, is very important. For all our colleagues, senior or junior, old or young, offering an opportunity to maintain a balanced life is one of the ways that large companies can hope to attract and retain good people in the future.

Jacob Wallenberg,
Chairman,
SE Banken Group

much more so than American business people do. Americans easily get caught up in the frenzied pace of business and often think nothing of working seven days, taking work home, answering e-mail at midnight. Europeans see the danger of losing balance and connection with one's self and one's family. They are willing to talk about it, to make it a priority within their companies. Balance of life is on their corporate agenda. Executive health is on the corporate agenda.

But regulating a balanced life is a bad idea. The European commission is tending toward mandating a thirty-five-hour workweek. **That is not going to work.** First of all, the thirty-five-hour week will drive up costs because factories, to remain competitive, will have to keep going; adding extra workers in addition to those already putting in overtime.

I believe we have to try role-modelling and education instead of legislation. We must make people aware of the importance of their own health—how it is valued in business as well as all aspects of life. We must make individuals, not states or governments, accountable for balance of life. A mandated workweek will not allow individuals to find balance: one that expresses their own personal structure. People who find their own balance are able to maintain productivity and contribute to a healthy culture.

8 A Leadership Agenda for the 21st Century

360 DEGREE INSIGHT

Remember the chief executive who came home one night to discover his son is a video game expert? Well, as he told us, "While I may be ignorant at times, I'm nobody's fool." A week after he'd tried his son's game and failed so miserably, he went home and marched right back into his son's room.

"How did you get so good?" he asked. It took a few repetitions of the question before his son realised that his father wasn't just complimenting him, that he really wanted to know. Finally, his son tried to answer:

"Dad, it's simple, I guess. Once you have the basic moves, you use them."

"But how do you always know which ones to use?" the executive asked. "How do you decide so fast?"

There are three things that I put in my own strategic plan for being successful in the new Europe. One, we need to think more in terms of non-material assets, like brand—the power of a brand—rather than material assets. The second is technology, and the third is the customer.

Marco Jesi,
President,
Frito-Lay Southern Europe

"Oh, that." The son picked up the control panel of his video game and thought a minute. He stared into the warm-up screen, a preview loop of the actual game that runs until the "Start Game" command is given. His father waited patiently for his ten-year-old wisdom.

"You can't just look at one thing," the son finally said. "You have to look at everything at once—kind of like sitting back and seeing the whole scene. If you get the whole screen picture then you don't waste your moves. Every move counts."

The father nodded and stared at the screen, not at all sure that he fully understood.

"You see, Dad, I've played enough now that I *know* the skills—you dodge, speed up, slow down, shoot, advance, retreat. But I have to relax my grip sometimes and look at the whole screen. That way, I can see the traps and changes, the approaching allies and enemies right away. I just do it without really thinking too hard about it and I guess I'm just more relaxed. So it seems like I'm ready for things before they happen. It's like I can sense them approaching! Weird, huh?"

With that, the father thanked his son, left him alone at his game, and went into his study, scratching his head. Something about what his son had said had struck home, but he wasn't clear on it yet. Then, like a flash of lightning, he got it. His business situation was the same. He was preoccupied with shooting all his missiles at the four warrior

> I think that people who are hung-up on their own ego are eventually hung-up on their own ego. That becomes all-important. You do not need a huge ego to be a successful individual.
>
> *Simon Merriman,*
> *Former Director,*
> *Connolly Luxury Goods*

men in the front of the screen without noticing the warships gathering on the far horizon.

A TIME FOR LEADERSHIP
PERSPECTIVES—THE BIGGER PICTURE

After several months of work in culture change with a particular European client, we received a call one day from the CEO. He said he had "a really big problem". So much had succeeded for him in recent months, we were intrigued. He had worked tirelessly in three separate countries to get his diverse team leaders and members on the same page—and his efforts had paid off. The teams were up and running, checking in with each other and with him on a weekly basis at least, sometimes daily.

Language and culture barriers had been addressed company-wide. Working on his own communications and leadership skills, he had changed his own behaviour. He never failed to initiate a direct contact he might previously have thought unnecessary. His example was increasingly felt and followed throughout the company. By all accounts, the culture was becoming healthier and more performance-focused than ever before. The financial shape of the company was improving steadily, too: His board was not only agreeing to his ideas and figures, they was excited about them.

> I am a believer that you can have a successful personal and business life without having to resort to this huge amount of egoism that people seem to think is the way you should project yourself to be successful. You can be successful and still be a nice person.
>
> *Simon Merriman,*
> *Former Director,*
> *Connolly Luxury Goods*

After he related to us his difficulty, we agreed that his problem was real and potentially very significant, but found that in comparison to the huge strides his people had made as an organisation, it was relatively minor. And it could have been worse. He could have noticed this key issue too late, after much greater damage had been done.

Learning to excel in the new European business environment will be a many-tiered process that will involve some good, old-fashioned mistake making. The process will involve adapting and refining.

That is precisely what had happened to this CEO. In the midst of his multi-level work in the field as well as in the boardroom, he had become tightly focused on day-to-day details. One day he had to take a brief flight between offices. In the air, he discovered how deep into the day-to-day leadership issues he had slipped. He read in the newspaper about a deal a competitor had recently completed with one of his legacy customers. The sudden realisation hit him that he had failed to come up for air long enough to notice an emerging business trend, and it knocked him for a loop. It was a critical miss. Not only would the deal have saved his company great expense, but it would have boosted the company's already improving revenue structure. Had he been alert, had he watched the horizon, he knew his group would have been in a position to take advantage of the opportunity first.

I think the real winners are going to be those who can combine strategic management with richly empowered local capacity; delivering within the overall context, making the maximum of local regional differences.

David Henshaw,
CEO,
Liverpool City Council

that the way for successful leaders to handle business is not to speed-up themselves, but to do what in fact appears to be the opposite. In order to move forward, leadership needs to slow down, take a step back, and gain perspective.

Stepping back means looking at the big picture, and taking the time to do it on a regular basis. By stepping away from the scattered fires that need putting out on a daily basis, we gain the essential perspective it takes to make even better decisions. It means letting up on the historically incessant call for leaders to maintain the appearance of *doing, doing, doing*, too often without regard for—or even knowledge of—the ever-changing big picture.

A key component of new leadership is technology. I am convinced that our Achilles heel preventing us from going further faster is that we don't yet have a common, integrated information system The more comfort we have with our KPI's, our key measures, the better we are at letting go and delegating. If we have the right people, and the right strategy, the right information, then we can let go. And letting go is critical in dealing with complexity.

Bill McLaughlin,
Former President & CEO,
Frito-Lay Europe

A NEW MILLENNIUM STARTS—THE "READY, AIM, FIRE" APPROACH ENDS

We have found, with the many clients we've been working with in Europe, that leaders in general are far too steeped in daily operational issues. As such, they can be clearly defined as working one level below their "job description". And when an entire management team works one step below the level they should be working on, big questions blink in figurative, warning, neon above the executive suite: "Who's watching the horizon? Who the heck is flying this plane?"

When leaders get wrapped up in the details of management, they fail to see some of the key strategic issues that are of critical "Game Over" importance for their company. Speed is a good thing; frenzy is not good! With his nose pressed against the glass, the leader will not be able to see the whole picture.

Stepping back allows us to scan the horizon, and it is such a critical element of leadership that it precedes all of the incremental elements of building a leadership agenda. To put it another way, we need a healthy "portal of perspective", one gained by shifting one's own position when necessary. Leaders need to be able to bring into focus the long, broad view. And they will have to gain information in a real and meaningful way. Assumptions based on yesterday's successes won't cut it on the 21st century playing field.

> There are characteristics of leadership that I put highly. One is strategic vision: a good leader has to have vision himself, rather than just a vision that is developed by a staff reporting to him. You have to have what I would describe as a 360 degree radar screen that will look over the horizon. You need to have humility. Some of the least-effective leaders have been those who have been too arrogant to admit when they were wrong.
>
> *Nigel Stapleton,*
> *Former Joint Chairman & CEO,*
> *Reed Elsevier*

HEY! HAVE YOU HEARD THIS ONE?

The key to gaining perspective is listening— deep listening with real curiosity and interest. And listening often goes counter to the behaviour and role of the traditional leader.

Filter Water, Not Information

The successful 21st century leader will invest serious MBWA (Management by Walking

Around) energy in order to gather information, to listen, and to learn what is truly going on within the organisation. And he or she must do it in a manner of heightened sensitivity and openness. This is crucial because only by being out and among colleagues, workers, and customers, can the leader access unfiltered information. Unfiltered information is the mother lode. This is real data mining, in the human sense. It is invaluable because it alone can generate new ideas, the very ideas that will be necessary for survival in the new environment. Unfiltered information creates the freedom and distance required to identify new levels of understanding, and ultimately, to set and reach new goals.

Filtered information, on the other hand, is laden with spins, reflecting agendas and assumptions. We colour the information with what we think we already know; what we think is a new insight is often really nothing more than *old* information in new clothes. Or, as a friend of mine says, "Some people's ideas are like old wine in new bottles: it looks good but doesn't taste that great."

> In today's environment, leadership creates a high degree of pressure. You are having to pull very different levers simultaneously—the lever of operational efficiency and the pure economic drivers; the lever of people and cultural dynamics; and then, the levers that relate to the regulatory and political environment.
>
> *Rupert Gavin,*
> *Chief Executive,*
> *BBC Worldwide*

THE LEADERSHIP AGENDA

The additional agenda for the 21st century must be a *leadership* agenda, not only a speeded-up *business-as-usual* agenda. Business-as-usual deals with traditional questions: "How do we get to market? How do we gain market share?" But this is not the only agenda that will take Europe where it needs to go. Business-as-usual is necessary, but no longer sufficient. We need an additional agenda on the table, and it can be built from five steps we have outlined below.

1) The Buck Starts Where It Used To Stop

In any kind of process, the one accountable place to begin is at the beginning, with oneself. Having stepped back and done what it takes to listen and truly observe his organisation and his or her own behaviour, the leader (and I suggest all senior executives) should undergo an unflinching self-examination. Today's CEO is going to lead an organisation through some of the hairiest, most disconcerting times since the creation of the first corporation. No one fully knows what will be afoot in coming years. Business school case studies of the future will be based upon the transitions we go through at this key juncture.

The CEO needs to assess his or her own health to ensure a life that is in balance. Physical conditioning is another personal assessment area that cannot be undervalued—a healthy body, diet, and mind are essential to active, successful leadership.

The leader must acquire *any* new skills necessary to function in this environment, be it

Keep flexible. Be prepared to change relatively quickly. We are a very consistent organisation, we have a plan, we have a strategy and we tend to execute to it and when there's road blocks we don't panic and we find a way round the road blocks and we still believe in that. But on the other hand the pace of change that is occurring I think means that all of us are going to have to be flexible as to how we move in and out of markets, how we move in and out of products and services and be prepared to bite the bullet. I'd say that flexibility and the ability to take that tough decision is going to be important.

Jim Wadia,
Worldwide Managing Partner,
Arthur Andersen

Everywhere you operate, anticipate your customers' expectations.

Baron Paul Buysse,
CEO,
Vickers plc

learning to navigate the Internet or addressing fundamentals of teamwork and communication technology in workshops and seminars. Resisting the wave of technology is a certain death sentence.

One CEO we interviewed, for example, took the importance of studying far beyond what most of us would consider standard business concerns. Rupert Gavin of BBC Worldwide began studying the history of the Catholic Church between the fourteenth and sixteenth centuries when looking for a parallel to his business situation—the problem of converting a public service organisation into a commercial one while trying to retain the public service features customers expect. He wants to heed the lesson he learned from studying the history of the Church, which suffered fragmentation during this period of transition.

Gavin sees the transition as critical to the BBC and recognises that if the big adjustment succeeds, it will be because leadership has taken the time to develop a culture that can effectively balance both the commercial and public service ethos of the business.

To establish a new leadership agenda in this time of rapid change and market expansion, European business leaders will have to take their concerns and the search for solutions to new lengths. They will have to be willing to work and study even in seemingly unrelated areas for answers. The tools of the past may no longer be as effective in 21st century European business as they where in the previous decade.

Listening, again, is key; it cannot be overemphasised. Leaders need to seek information and be open to receiving it honestly. How often do executives get feedback on personal issues? Possibly the board has supplied such information in the past. But what about the staff giving direct and honest feedback? The old model holds that the senior executives have "made it", and no longer need to learn or change. The sooner such stale rubbish is incinerated, the better. It is never too late to seek a variety of viewpoints, to learn, or to change. And never before has learning and adaptability on the part of leadership been more necessary.

2) No Loose Linkage: Build a Senior Team

With the importance of personal development and the Shadow of the Leader established, we need to focus on the crucial role that the leadership team must play in building and improving culture, and therefore, competitive performance. The first step is to understand every aspect of our team(s) as they exist and to make corrections where necessary. Some of the questions to ask, and continually reassess, are:

❖ What are my team's strengths and weaknesses?
❖ Which team members get along and why? Which do *not* and why?

> Gone are the days that you can have the single-minded chief executive. The characteristics of a successful chief executive, I am pretty convinced, are an extraordinary array of different talents and sensitivities. But a key one is listening.
>
> *Rupert Gavin,*
> *Chief Executive,*
> *BBC Worldwide*

❖ Do I clearly understand the strengths and weaknesses of our corporate culture?

❖ Are we aligned on our leadership role(s) in building a high-performance culture?

❖ If we spend more time fighting over budgets than arriving at solid solutions, chances are we are just as dysfunctional in other areas. What are they? How can these areas be improved?

❖ The fundamental question always is: "How can we work better as a team?"

3) Champion the Culture at All Times

In order to create a healthy, high-performance culture, leaders must continually concern themselves with their people, recognise performance, and make examples of people who are fulfilling the overall goals of the company. Strong, direct action must be taken in favour of culture. A sure way to set the tone for that to happen is to base executive compensation on how well each team member disseminates company values down through the organisation. How well each team member *walks the talk* will directly affect the soundness of the culture.

Leaders will have to take every opportunity—and create more—to build healthy cultures. That means continually drumming the message, and then repeating it. Here's how serious it is: Companies will have to spend significantly more

We can work smarter and better and are desperately looking for how to operationalise that design. It is all very well having the aspiration, but I think a leader has to figure out how to operationalise. You have to help people operationalise what you are talking about and be specific about what that means. Leadership has been too heavily skewed in recent years toward visions and not enough toward making it happen.

Martin Glenn,
President & CEO,
Walkers Snack Foods

Rather than circle the drain of regret over his error, the leader thought about what had happened and what he could do about it. His leadership responsibility was to provide a working example, to walk the talk; but he also had to remain at the helm. Leadership was his domain on all levels now, no longer limited to the important tactical management issues. The crux of his challenge was clear: engender viable teams, a healthy culture, and a competitive edge *while* identifying new strategies and seizing timely opportunities. How? He needed to add an even more elusive leadership skill: seeing the broader perspective, the bigger picture!

A TIME… TO STEP BACK?

The trends toward globalisation and acceleration make the current time a critical one for improving leadership throughout the organisation. For CEOs and top managers, this is the time to *make time* to develop and, if necessary, create our own leadership skills. Putting solid leadership skills into practice has never been more important. In practicing, we will discover and change as quickly as we need to. And we need to, quickly.

In this book, we have tried to make clear the idea that successful leadership in the 21st century takes place multidimensionally. We have stressed

If there's one course all executives should take, it's listening skills. You've got to be able to get people to open up and tell you their fears, concerns, or what's really deep-down nagging them about what it is we're trying to do. You've got to get them on board in a way that makes them comfortable. To do that, you've got to listen, and I think most executives are terrible listeners

Robert Binney,
Managing Director,
Citibank N.A.

money on development and training for supervisors and the hourly work force. To me, it is staggering to see how common it is in Europe for companies to spend thousands and thousands on executive seminars and training retreats, but next to nothing, comparatively, on front-line employees. Spending the money to train supervisors and lower-level staff, to take that extra step to drive the organisation's message home, pays off tremendously, beyond what most people expect. It is an incredible boon to aligning the culture with the organisation's goals.

Key questions to ask continually are:

❖ Where is the culture weak and where is it strong?

❖ Do our culture and brand match?

❖ How well are we communicating the values and behaviours that make up the culture?

❖ Do employees understand the linkage between our culture and competitive advantage?

❖ How often do we celebrate success?

Newsletters and internal Web pages are excellent tools for carrying forward the message of culture, so long as the CEO and senior team live the ideas set forth in them. In newsletters, Web pages, and company television programmes, leaders can express and re-emphasise the organisation's values; how the company defines success. They can outline short-term goals and recognise those people who have

Michael Porter, in his book *Competitive Advantage of Nations,* talks about the issue of change being the great catalyst for development. The advances of technology are transforming every business, so business leaders have to be familiar with the basic tools of change, many of which are related to communication technology.

Peter Sutherland,
Chairman & MD,
Goldman Sachs International

aligned themselves with the brand and moved the company that much further toward its goals.

4) Apply The Five Principles Of Leadership Set Forth In This Book

In the final analysis, good leadership is not about style. It is about substance. While we don't have all the answers yet, we interviewed a great many business leaders in Europe at the brink of the new millennium and arrived at the principles contained in this book. They are as follows:

❖ Distributed Leadership: Leadership is no longer the realm of a select few at the top, but must be distributed down through the organisation;

❖ Culture Impacts Performance: A healthy culture impacts performance in a positive way;

❖ Culture Is the Brand: Brand and culture must match;

❖ Shadow of the Leader(s): The organisation will reflect the behaviours of the leader and the senior management team;

❖ Balance of Life: Those in leadership positions must achieve a balanced life to be successful and make the company so.

You have always had a real variety of types that seem to be successful. Contrast Patton and Montgomery. Patton was as nutty as a fruitcake, from what I can tell, but still very successful. Montgomery was much more conservative, straight down the line, and also very successful. So I guess they did some common things well.

Martin Glenn,
President & CEO,
Walkers Snack Foods

Take It to the Board

Lastly, it is crucial to elevate this leadership agenda to the boardroom. The leadership agenda for the 21st century is surely as critical as strategy, financial agenda, budgets, technology, and organisational structure. It is not an agenda for one or two isolated managers within the organisation, but a key for every member of the organisation.

> The CEO will have to pay more attention than in the past to the human factor and to developing leadership skills among his key associates. So he will no longer be the only leader, but rather a leader of leaders.
>
> *Lode Beckers,*
> *Chairman,*
> *Lobo n.v.*

9 Staying Open for Business in the New Europe

A SUMMARY

Out of the rubble of the Berlin Wall has emerged a Europe where the driving forces are not ideology and politics anymore, but business and technology. The institution of the European Union, the Euro, deregulation, cross-trading, open borders, and global competition have created a revolutionary business climate. The Fortress Europe of protectionism and nationalistic cartels is being challenged by the Web-speed business tactics of spirited entrepreneurs; the Internet generation that travels anywhere and everywhere to create a global market. Companies, not nations, are weaving a real continental economy, and mergers and acquisitions are redefining the European landscape.

Unless old business in new Europe can become globally competitive—quickly—it will be out-priced, out-produced, and left out of the

A year ago we were still thinking of traditional manufacturing in our region, even though there is over-capacity in the marketplace.. We were hoping in two or three years time demand would increase. But the whole marketplace has changed; you can't get near the costs of production that are being put together in the Far East. So we are having to think completely differently about a new industrial base.

David Henshaw,
CEO,
Liverpool City Council

larger marketplace. European companies must quickly learn to do business differently in order to cut costs, improve quality, and reduce the time it takes to get products to market.

THE ELEVENTH HOUR WAKE-UP CALL

The real task before today's chief executive and senior executive team, then, is to figure out ways they can quickly learn the new skills needed to lead and manage in 21st century Europe. Old business skills such as planning, organising, staffing, directing, and controlling are merely foundation points. Now Europe's CEOs are faced with new and more complex boards and government bodies; multiple markets and more competitors than ever; multicultural stakeholders; and employees who live in different countries and speak multiple languages.

We need new principles on which to base a substantively new style of functioning. This book is titled *A Time for Leadership* because only a new kind of leadership can galvanize and transcend the great complexities in the new European work force and marketplace. The principles of leadership are the foundation of that new leadership.

The old-style leadership within Fortress Europe, developed over many decades on a country-by-country basis, was characterised by

Intrusive control of all activities within any organisation is no longer feasible or desirable.

Peter Sutherland,
Chairman & MD,
Goldman Sachs International

To distribute leadership, the CEO must begin by changing himself or herself by getting rid of the *buck-stops-here* notion of lone accountability. The CEO's most important function is to have, foster, promote, and validate open and supportive relationships. This builds trust, empowers people, releases creative energy and spirit, and distributes leadership throughout the organisation. It develops a culture that dialogues possibilities rather than debates impossibilities.

The current European business atmosphere is starving for relationship power, because the internal changes that are required to adapt quickly to the Web-speed environment can only come about with the ability to build and understand relationships. From now on, extraordinary results will require extraordinary relationships. Business is not separate from human beings; it *is* human beings, and strong relationships are a powerful currency.

Public speaking and media skills are important, but I actually think that one-on-one skills are very important as well; maybe more important.

Nigel Stapleton,
Former Joint Chairman & CEO,
Reed Elsevier

In the Distributed Leadership model, information flows through a network in many directions at once, not just up to the boss and back down. This results in better-informed, more innovative decisions. Everybody shares resources and talks across the system.

Distributed Leadership raises the bar and requires everyone, from the CEO on down, to be innovative, reflective, and introspective. It makes it OK to stop and think; OK to ask the most important questions, such as, "Why not?"

and "What if?" Leadership is not about management teams; it is about everybody in the organisation leading.

CULTURE DIRECTLY
IMPACTS PERFORMANCE

Without a doubt, the collective ideas and beliefs of the people shape the behaviours of the place—the habits, customs, and the tacit as well as stated rules the company uses to meet its goals successfully.

These beliefs and behaviours comprise the corporate culture. And more than anything, the culture, "the way we do things around here", determines company results. This organisational personality is strong enough to make or break a strategic plan, a long-range goal, or simple day-to-day operations. If the culture is stuck in habitual one-way thinking, where management doesn't embrace or even listen to ideas from the ranks, you can bet that the culture is one in which people don't speak up, where meetings don't start on time, or just get cancelled at the last minute. Morale is low, tardiness is high, and overall performance is in a constant slump.

To meet the demands of competition in New Europe, executives must focus on customer service, speed to market, brand diversification; a more pan-European, and ultimately, more global

I believe the successful leaders in tomorrow's Europe will need a European mindset. My background is completely international—I was born in Switzerland, my father was half-Belgian and my mother is what we used to call Russian; actually she is half-Ukrainian and half from a family of German-origin Balts who lived in Estonia. I did my MBA in France, and now I live in the UK.

Helen Alexander,
CEO,
The Economist Group

posture. When the strategy is agreed upon, ide-ally the culture implements it. Calamity befalls the company that attempts a new strategy with a petrified culture stuck in old ways. Imagine a world-class racing boat trying to compete while towing a freighter.

Culture determines how much productive, imaginative, and innovative thinking the organ-isation gets from its people. It is the competitive edge. High-quality people want to work in healthy, high-performance cultures. When a company is a fantastic place to work, it attracts the top talent.

Leadership cannot expect its people to behave in a different way unless its people begin to think in a different way. To nurture the culture, leader-ship has to nurture new thinking—beginning with a viable set of values such as trust, respect, teamwork, accountability, support, and feedback.

A healthy culture focuses on the customer. No matter what our nationalities are, no matter what our old cultures have been, adjusting our focus to the customer lets us see that we are all trying to accomplish the same thing. With this focus, the momentum killers of internal politics and office-envy diminish. Morale crushers like tardiness, cancelled meetings, incomplete pro-jects, and the lack of new ideas, disappear. Deci-sions are easier, and there is less posturing over "our way" versus "their way", or the need to make sure "A" doesn't step on "B's" toes. Feed-

I believe the CEO of the new European companies will have to work on four areas: globalisation trends, innovation require-ments, corporate culture, and creating a sense of entrepreneurship for employees. People need to feel they have a certain freedom to make things happen.

Hugo Vandamme,
President & CEO,
Barco N.V.

back from the marketplace arrives quicker, and adjustments are made quickly and smoothly.

When we speak about culture and performance, we are not just talking about getting the good numbers, but about customer service, new ideas, the spirit that attracts new talent, and an environmentally stimulating situation providing growth. Business *is* about making money, but that is not the only measure of success. Work has to become more than just a place to work. It's a place to learn, to hone our skills, and to satisfy our basic human need to make a difference.

> The additional responsibilities of the CEO in the New Europe will be to inspire his organisation to even higher levels.
>
> *Kees Storm,*
> *Chairman, Executive Board,*
> *Aegon N.V.*

YOUR CULTURE IS YOUR BRAND

Brand has evolved into a large-scale, complex communication process that can add value to the corporation. It no longer differentiates a product's effectiveness; it differentiates a corporation's vision, goals, and effective presence in the world.

External branding effectively gets the word out and raises expectations in the customer's mind. Internal branding leads the corporate culture to behaviours that resonate with and thereby deliver the brand. **Culture is the Brand**. This is a revolutionary principle. Only when the brand image is mirrored by the company culture can the brand deliver what the customer expects from the company. If the brand promise is *not* mirrored by the culture, the customer's expectations are frustrated and he feels manipulated by the company.

Our culture is our brand. It is what the customer actually experiences, first and last. It is live interaction with the organic make-up of the company, the people-to-people encounters that leave an indelible mark. If my company's brand promises friendly and efficient service, then everyone in the company, from the boardroom to the broom closet, must define, promote, and live-out the best attributes of friendship. We behave this way not because it makes us feel better or makes everybody look attractive, but because these behaviours create the culture that delivers the brand that keeps the customer coming back. It is as plain as that—and vital to the survival of the business.

When brand expectations and culture clash, the effects can devastate business. When brand and culture *match,* the effects can devastate the competition. If we experience less than we expect, disappointment sets in like a bad cold. And because of the vast array of competitors out there, most of us don't return to the source of disappointment: We go elsewhere. But when we interact with a human being within a company and the brand comes alive, there is integrity; a fusion of culture and brand that produces a kind of energy that we call satisfaction.

If leadership empowers employees to deliver results to the customer, then they will deliver the

The history of Carlsberg is a story of quality. It is not just total quality management, it is the Carlsberg culture.

Flemming Lindeløv,
President & CEO,
Carlsberg A/S

culture that delivers the kind of service expected from the brand advertising. This creates customer satisfaction and loyalty. And when this is the case, the financial outcome can be astounding. A 5 percent increase in customer loyalty can produce profit increase from 25 percent to 85 percent.

The task of leadership is to build a culture that is the living spirit of our brand—through leadership behaviour, supportive policies that empower employees, role modelling, behavioural standards that mirror the brand, and constant communication. Most importantly, leaders must see themselves as part of the culture they want to create. If we are going to lead the culture to shift its habitual behaviours, then we must begin by changing our own habits and behaviours or change will not take place.

THE LEADER'S SHADOW TOUCHES EVERY CORNER OF THE ORGANISATION

> A strong culture will lead to strong brand. It's the promise of a positive experience when I see those Golden Arches that make loyal customers.
>
> *Paul Preston,*
> *Chairman,*
> *McDonald's UK*

What happens throughout the company mirrors the top. The corollary is that performance cannot be mandated; it must be led. The leader's personality and behaviour are an unfailing presence that does not require conscious adaptation or acceptance to exist; the leader's shadow, his cast of influence, simply is.

Leadership is not about continual debate. You sometimes have to take the tough decisions that maybe not everyone in the organisation at that time agrees with. I was born in Ireland, and I happen to believe the minority is normally right. Because when everyone agrees with something, it's either already happened or you are too late. So leadership is all about going out there and actually convincing people that the path is the right way to go. Because it isn't obvious. The important breakthroughs in any business are not the ones that were obvious at the time.

Neville Isdell,
President,
Coca-Cola Beverages plc

We need to be conscious of how the leadership shadow creates the culture. The leader may be a great idea person, but if he doesn't exhibit hands on skills or follow through, then those he motivates with his ideas will do the same—have ideas but no follow-through. A leader who arrives late can have the most strictly worded tardiness policies ever devised, yet his people will not value punctuality.

Leadership is a finely woven collabouration at all levels. But in European business now, there is a deep gulf between the senior board and everybody else. Bridging it will do no less than make or break our ability to participate in the global marketplace. This is a critical challenge facing companies at the start of the new millennium.

The shadow of the leader, in the speeded-up Europe of the 21st century, has got to cast itself more positively, profoundly, and multidimensionally than ever before. Because it is impossible to address verbally and instantly all the areas that require leadership in the new environment, the leader's influence must cross traditional boundaries and enter the Information Age. The CEO must be influential and multidimensional enough to engender leadership down through the organisation. And that cannot be done in memo or meeting form or by issuing directives. To quote Warren Bennis, "A leader doesn't just get the message across, a leader *is* the message."

heavy monopolies, subsidies, a captive market-place, and a restricted work force. The principle of "Authority Equals Power" produced strong centralised leadership and centralised bureaucra-cies. In the new global marketplace, where there is a fast flow of capital, goods, and labour, and where labour and consumers speak different lan-guages and value different traditions, autocratic leadership principles cannot provide the neces-sary leverage, nor the speed of decision-making at the local level that is necessary for competitive success. So much new information travels via the Internet at fantastic speed every hour that no one leader can access or process it.

DISTRIBUTE THE LEADERSHIP; EXPERIENCE THE WISDOM

If real leadership—with its incumbent responsi-bilities and accountabilities—can be shared, by way of rapport and open relationships among talented team members, and distributed through the corporate culture, then the possibilities for growth, flexibility, and success are innumerable.

This is the new principle of **Distributed Lead-ership,** or Distributed Wisdom. The role of the CEO becomes one of influence, not control. He or she is an agent of change and adaptability in a world that is radically mutable, preparing more people for bigger leadership roles in the company.

What is happening in Europe is that European companies are becoming more American and possi-bly, we will see American companies adopt some of the European corpo-rate culture. European companies of all sizes have become much more focused, effective, and professional in the way they run their business. They have clear strategies and top-class manage-ment. The networks that have been so dominant and tightly-knit, where CEOs know each other and have gone to school together, will never again be as important as profes-sional management and leadership skills.

Antonia Ax:son Johnson,
Chairman,
The Axel Johnson Group

Every CEO and all leadership teams must either walk their talk or deal with terrible situations of slumping morale and low productivity. When salaries are cut everywhere except on the top tier; when teams are set up for effective implementation but don't get along—or even meet; or when any major change is requested but not modelled by leadership, employees will be reticent, even resentful, of change themselves. They will keep real concerns hidden. They won't speak up at meetings. They'll contribute no positive ideas.

CEOs and senior teams must confront their own behaviours in order to cast a positive shadow. They must commit to address any and all issues and concerns with each other, rather than with *any* third party; to represent a unified team to the organisation; to be supportive of each other, at all times; and, most critically, to engage in healthy debate to work to reach alignment and to support the group decision once it is reached.

If the world is changing too fast and most companies have more competition, then the senior team had better work on the culture and their its own leadership.

Jan Froeshaug,
Group President and CEO,
Egmont International Holding
A/S

Understanding the importance of the leader's influence, and adopting the necessary behaviours, will be the passage to the multidimensionality required of the 21st century leader. The vastness of the new environment must be shared. Leaders who cast the appropriate shadow will create thriving cultures where all people in the company commit acts of positive leadership.

I think it's amazing how much more you can do if you are organised. If you go at it with a sense of purpose, have some fun, then you can do remarkably well and have a balance in life.

David Thorpe,
*Vice President Global Operations
Information Solutions,
EDS*

A BALANCED LIFE IS A HEALTHY AND PRODUCTIVE LIFE

This principle saves the leader from himself. Every human being is more productive when in a balanced state of physical and psychological well-being. For the business leader in particular, achieving a personal balance results in highly valued capabilities—good listening, broad perspective, clear thinking, innovative ideas, and wisdom.

Having time and energy for all the things that are important to us in life makes us relaxed, rested, flexible, and optimistic. Our minds remain open and uncluttered so that ideas can bubble up from their buried places. To put it another way, we can more easily access our higher capabilities when our anxiety, fatigue, and agitation are out of the way.

Every leader must make personal health and balance a priority in the 21st century. Without it, one's life at home and at work will creak and break from the strain. Even though balance is a tricky thing to achieve and is different for everybody, the CEO must make it a priority, or it won't happen. His or her health and effectiveness, and that of everyone in the organisation, depend on it. When the leader models personal balance and well-being, then those around him or her will do the same. Eventually, balance is valued throughout the organisation.

As leaders, we have to train ourselves to

become aware of out-of-balance indicators and recognise them early. We must check in on ourselves daily: "How am I emotionally, physically, mentally?" Seek feedback on a regular basis from the sources around us—our spouses, our children, and our friends, our colleagues: "Do you think I am being effective here? Is there something you see that I don't see?" Then we have to be willing to hear what they're going to tell us.

When each of us looks at our own life, we can determine priorities that help us preserve and maintain our balance of life. Family, art, music, theatre, travel, study, exercise, diet, social time with friends other than business contacts, meditation, hobbies—any and all of the things that bring us joy and meaning must find a place in our life. Once our time is allocated to tasks and activities that can bring us balance, we will need only one other tool: Be Here Now.

When I am Here Now, I empty my mind of all else except what I am concentrating on at the moment. I pour myself 100 percent into the present moment. When I'm in conversation with my spouse, I am 100 percent there; when I'm listening to a presentation at work, I am 100 percent there; when I am bicycling a country road, I am 100 percent there. This ability increases my effectiveness because I am focused, concentrated, and get more done with less repetition, confusion, and wasted energy.

No one is going to *hand* the leader, or any

To be honest, it's very difficult to balance my personal and professional life. We work too hard— eighty to ninty hours a week. It's ridiculous, but I don't see how we can do it differently. Looking for balance, I might have to say, "OK, maybe I don't now control the whole file for the meeting tomorrow, but it is 10:00 PM and I want to spend some time with my wife and my children." I try to keep my Sundays clear and I deliberately try to be on all kinds of associations/foundations so that I'm not just focused on banking and financial matters all the time.

Dolf van den Brink,
Member of the Board,
ABN Amro Holding N.V.

busy person, the time it takes to include the things that create balance. The business certainly won't make time for anyone. It is a living organism with its own unending appetites and demands. Each of us has to create the mindset and time to include things in the course of each day that keep us balanced and effective.

TAKING IT TO THE LIMIT

The 21st century agenda must be a leadership agenda, not just a business-as-usual agenda. Today's CEO is going to lead an organisation through the most disconcerting times since the creation of the first corporation. Future business-school case studies will be based upon the transitions we go through now. For CEOs and top managers, this is a time to make time to develop, or if necessary, create our own leadership skills. But most importantly, we won't get anywhere in this new environment unless we accept that from this point on; learning to excel will be a multi-tiered process that will require good, old-fashioned mistake-making. And it will not preclude having to adapt and refine new behaviours.

In this book, we have tried to clearly establish that successful leadership in the 21st century will take place multidimensionally. We have shown that though the world has accelerated, the way for the successful leader to handle busi-

> There will be less protectionism. It will be a much more competitive environment. And competitive not only in the field where you operate, but also competitive to get the right people.
> *Vagn Holck Andersen, Chairman, Interdan A/S*

ness is not to speed-up him-/herself, but to do what in fact appears to be the opposite. In order to move forward, leadership needs to take a step back to slow down!

Stepping back means taking the time to look at everything. By stepping away from the scattered fires that erupt every day, we gain the desperately needed perspective it takes to make the best, right decisions. It means letting up on the historically incessant call for leaders to maintain the appearance of *doing, doing, doing*, too often without regard for—or even knowledge of—the ever-changing big picture. Contrary to traits senior managers have revered and striven toward for decades, cutting-edge 21st century leadership will be less hectic.

The new leader will acquire new skills necessary to function, be it learning to navigate the Internet, or addressing fundamentals of teamwork and communication technology in workshops and seminars. He or she will develop the ability to listen with curiosity, sensitivity, and interest. This goes counter to the exalted ego role of the traditional leader. Leaders must seek information and be open to receiving it honestly.

The CEO will focus on the crucial role that the leadership team plays in building and improving culture, and therefore, competitive performance. And, speaking of culture, the 21st century leaders will continually concern themselves with their people; recognising performance and

> The biggest difficulty I had in moving up from CFO to Chief Executive was that the CFO's function is far more action-orientated. As CFO, you change your currency profile, your view on interest rates, your debt maturity profile; there are lots of reporting deadlines to meet. The biggest difficulty in moving from CFO to CEO is that the most important thing about the Chief Executive job is "think more and act less".
>
> *Nigel Stapleton,*
> *Former Joint Chairman & CEO,*
> *Reed Elsevier*

When the sea was calm, all
ships showed mastership in
floating.
William Shakespeare

It is only during the storm
that we truly become sailors.
*John R. Childress,
Chief Executive,
Senn-Delaney Leadership*

making examples of people who are fulfiling the overall goals of the company. They will take strong, direct action in favour of culture; continually drumming the message, then repeating it. They will continually ask: "How healthy is the culture?"; "Does the brand and culture match?"; "Are we communicating with the culture?" Companies will spend money on supervisors and average workers, not just on executive seminars and training retreats.

A leadership agenda for the 21st century is as critical as strategic plans or financial plans, and it must be on the table at board meetings. It is not an agenda for one or two isolated managers within the organisation, but a key for every member of the organisation. The time for leadership is NOW!

Index

About Senn-Delaney
Leadership

The Senn-Delaney Leadership Consulting Group was founded in 1978 with a specific mission: Assist CEOs and senior executives to create High-performance Teams and Winning Cultures. Today, Senn-Delaney Leadership is a global firm known for its experience and accomplishments in the areas of Culture-Shaping, Team-building and Leadership Development. While management consultants work on formulating strategy, structure, systems, and processes, we as leadership consultants focus on creating the organisational and team effectiveness needed to ensure those change initiatives work.

High-performance teams and winning cultures are of utmost importance today. Research and experience confirm that the shortfall in most change initiatives is due to the human issues, not the technical ones. This is true for mergers, new leaders, new strategies, restructures, IT installations and all other major changes.

For over 20 years, we've worked with corporate leaders in the Energy, Information Technology, Financial Services, and Consumer Products/Diversified industries. Our clients include: Agilent, Toys "R" Us, Bell Atlantic, Pacific Bell, Sprint, British Telecom, British Gas, Commonwealth Edison, Portland General Electric, Florida Power and Light, Compaq Computer, IBM PC Division, Hewlett Packard, McDonald's U.S., PepsiCo, Bank One, GTE Information Services and Rockwell International. We have also aided the merger and acquisition transition process within organizational recombinations such as: Chemical-Chase Bank, Ohio Edison-Centerion, Southwestern Bell-Pacific Bell Directory, Compaq-Digital, and Bank One, First Chicago, and National Bank of Detroit.

As we approach and enter the new millennium, the professionals of the Senn-Delaney Leadership Consulting Group remain committed to our vision of "Making a Difference Through Leadership™."

For additional information about the consulting services of Senn-Delaney Leadership, please visit our website at: www.senndelaneyleadership.com.

SENN-DELANEY LEADERSHIP
Part of the Provant Solution
3780 Kilroy Airport Way, Long Beach, CA 90806
Phone (562) 426-5400
Fax (562) 426-5174